D0778339

# THE POWER OF APPRECIATION

## A New Approach to Personal and Relational Healing

— ❖ —

ADRIAN VAN KAAM
and
SUSAN MUTO

158.1
VAN

CROSSROAD · NEW YORK

1993

The Crossroad Publishing Company
370 Lexington Avenue, New York, NY 10017

Printed in the United States of America

**Library of Congress Cataloging-in-Publication Data**

Van Kaam, Adrian L., 1920–
    The power of appreciation : a new approach to personal and
relational healing / Adrian van Kaam and Susan Muto.
      p.  cm.
    Includes bibliographical references.
    ISBN 0-8245-1208-1 (pbk.)
    1. Gratitude. 2. Attitude (Psychology) 3. Conduct of life.
4. Gratitude—Religious aspects. 5. Attitude (Psychology)—
Religious aspects. 6. Spiritual life. I. Muto, Susan Annette.
II. Title.
BF575.G68V36  1993
158'.1—dc20

                                        92-25747
                                          CIP

# Contents

# Acknowledgments

**M**any appreciative people have shown us by the quality of their lives what this book attempts to describe through formative teachings and personal testimonies. Brave people who survived the horror of war, the shock of illness, the loneliness of aging, the pain of dislocation — some named, many unnamed — inspired its contents. Memories of family members, friends, students, and colleagues live again in these pages, at times cited but always present between the lines. Many times during the coauthoring process, we found our hearts uplifted in prayer and gratitude to God for mediating the message of divine love and mercy through their presence. We thank sincerely our supporters in the Epiphany Association, who in great measure made the dream of this book a reality. They enabled us to field test many of its ideas and confirmed that the practice of the power of appreciation benefits one both physically and spiritually, balancing the psyche and breaking the penchant for low-grade depression we all sometimes feel. Here we offer heartfelt thanks to our loyal staff, especially to our administrative assistant, Marilyn Russell, whose help and skill in realizing the final manuscript were invaluable, and to Barbara O'Day and Maria Muto, who contributed so much to the production effort. May all of them and every one of you be graced abundantly with the joy and peace of appreciative living.

*The emergence*

*of self*

*is*

*a*

*continuous event.*

*We*

*never arrive;*

*we are*

*always*

*arriving.**

---

*This affirmation and those found at the beginning of each chapter are texts
from two of our coauthored books, *The Emergent Self* and *The Participant Self*.

# Introduction

## by Adrian van Kaam

**I** am pleased to make available in this book coauthored by Dr. Susan Muto a proven approach to personal and relational healing: the power of appreciation. It has changed the lives of many people.

Take Steven McDonald, a police officer in his thirties, whose story appeared in the May 13, 1990, issue of *Parade Magazine*. His life seemed doomed after he was shot in New York City's Central Park in 1986. He was not expected to live since the wounds afflicted by his assailant paralyzed him from the neck down. Once a strong, independent man, he now had no choice but to depend on his family, friends, and neighbors for everything. Were it not for his own spirit and the love and support of his young wife, he would never have survived to become a national Father of the Year, an officer of the law hailed by dozens of organizations and honored by the president of the United States.

What was the secret of Steve's amazing recovery? What was the meaning of his having to spend the rest of his life in a wheelchair? He says in the book recounting his experiences that the most important thing in life is "people giving of themselves." He believes that what one person does for another is what ignites a whole people. There is for Steven yet another word that says it all, a word he directs mainly to the woman he will never again be able to hug, the word "thanks." On Valentine's Day he sent his wife, Patti Ann, a dozen roses with the words: "You have my eternal love and thanks for teaching me about love and life."

For many people, "thanks" is a word that has seen them through many traumatic experiences. In my own life I had to give thanks for the "blessing of a coronary." That was what I came to call my heart attack in 1980. It prompted me to try to condense in this book forty years of research and practice rooted in the power of appreciation. Appreciation rooted in faith helped me to survive the horrendous Hunger Winter of 1944–45 in the West of Holland during World War II. Circumstances forced me as a young seminarian cut off from my community to engage in a kind of emergency counseling for people hiding from deportation, suffering famine, agonizing over the loss of relatives in concentration camps, and facing grave uncertainty about the future. To help them I had to evolve a way of thinking that went beyond what mere psychology had to offer. Abstract answers to the whys and wherefores of human existence were of minimal help to people trying to maintain a sense of meaning in the midst of the dreadful losses confronting them daily.

In my search for ways to meet their needs, I gained new insights into the connections between mind and mood, one's state of life and one's coping ability. I observed that things worsened considerably if people lost the power of appreciation or if they were ignorant of the impact negative, depreciative thinking had on the way in which they spent their waking hours. Instead of giving direction *to* their lives, they were unconsciously directed *by* the influences pressing down *on* their lives.

What was happening in their surroundings gave shape and form to their inner selves and their relationships in optimistic or pessimistic ways. If they did not know how to appreciate any small moment that could brighten their heart and lift their spirits, they soon sunk into despair. They missed the proper mental and physical defenses that would prevent hostile people and adverse events from sapping their energy, depleting their aspirations, and maybe costing them their lives. Having lost the sense of appreciation for themselves and the good things of life, they seemed obsessed by depreciative thoughts that in the end proved to be debilitating. I tried to lift their spirits by talking with them about the power of praise and appreciation for anything praiseworthy in themselves, in others, and in their surroundings, no matter how small. These conversations gave me the intuition that one fruit of our suffering should be the initiating of a science of formation and appreciation. Many lonely people who came to me in their despondency inspired me to lay the foundations of this discipline.

My war experiences stayed with me when I engaged in postwar research and study in the fields of pedagogy and andragogy (child and adult development) at the Hoogveld Institute of the University of Nijmegen. In outlining the limits of what I learned there I was able to formulate better how my discipline of transcendent formation would be necessary to complement the findings of developmental, clinical, social, and educational disciplines. When I came to the United States, to teach at Duquesne University in Pittsburgh and to complete my doctoral study in clinical psychology at Case Western Reserve University in Cleveland, I sought further training in these two related fields at the University of Chicago, at the Alfred Adler Institute, and at Brandeis University. All of these occasions of study and practice made me increasingly aware of the need for a science of transcendent formation, first as a professor of psychology at Duquesne, and later as founder and director of the graduate Institute of Formative Spirituality. Both in the psychology department and in the institute, I was able to test rigorously the appreciative bent of the personality theory that is at the basis of this book. The results of these pioneering efforts were published in numerous books and articles and field tested at the ecumenical lay formation center in Pittsburgh, the Epiphany Association, I cofounded with Dr. Susan Muto in 1979.

During a two-year project (1987–89) with the chaplain corps of the United States Navy, Dr. Muto and I headed an Epiphany-sponsored team that had the chance to do extensive field work in an effort to integrate spiritual formation and pastoral care. We concluded that impotence in the realm of appreciative thinking and living has a deleterious effect on one's personal and professional capacity to care. It signals a disturbance in the ability to appraise one's life as ultimately meaningful rather than as ultimately meaningless.

Joyless people see the world and themselves in somber rather than subtle tones. This negative turn of thought, feeling, imagination, and perception affects the direction in which a person's life proceeds. Unless this depleting state of dis-ease is caught and reversed in time, it can lead to severe depression and an overall depreciative approach to life.

Depreciation saps our power to function effectively in the round of everyday events. We feel overwhelmed by problems, the victim of a mean world instead of a willing participant in its better aspects. This narrow vision can even produce a kind of impotence in the realm of the spirit, an inability to tap the resources of joy and energy hidden in everydayness. Many outstanding representatives of the medical, neurological, psychotherapeutic, social, educational, and clinical sciences have studied the conditions, dynamics, and effects of positive thinking on people. In accordance with the focus of these sciences, they limit themselves to the pretranscendent or quasitranscendent (gnostic) realm of life. We believe that the study of the postgnostic, fully transcendent horizon offers a new view of and gives a great boost to what we call our power of praise and appreciation.

Later experience and research confirmed these intuitions. Over the years we have been able to refine and test our theory. Observation of and experience with people in all walks of life suggest that we can learn to assess appreciatively rather than depreciatively the transcendent directives that come to us from daily experience. A glance at the Appendix at the end of the book will amply prove this point.

By developing the courage of candor in regard to the people and events that influence us, we can find new avenues of harmony between ourselves and the world around us. Our life will become more congenial and compatible. Moments of joy and serenity will begin to increase, even in the midst of setbacks and sufferings.

A first step toward initiating such change entails understanding the richness and depth of the power of appreciation. That of which we speak goes far beyond mere techniques of positive thinking and human development, even beyond the admittedly excellent insights of cognitive therapy. This approach to inner and outer healing touches upon the core of what it means to be distinctively human. It reminds me of a remarkable letter published on February 27, 1988, in the *New York Times*. It was tagged by the editors, "At the end, we ask the unanswerable questions all over again." Here are Anna's reflections in full:

To the Editor:

Am I the woman described in "At 85, Frightened by a Loss of Power" (Op-Ed, Jan. 31)? I certainly share with her the disabilities of old age, but I don't think either of my daughters would write to a newspaper about how irritating they find me. I walk with a cane, and my hands are swollen with arthritis. I frequently can't understand what my children are talking about. I have tried to answer my telephone when only the one on television was ringing. I've lost my Christmas card list and found it again under a pile of solicitations. I've helped save the whales, avert nuclear holocaust, end support of the contras. I've landed on a lot of mailing lists. I read everything they send me.

My personal correspondence has dwindled because many of my old correspondents are dead, and my children are busy with their own affairs. The solicitations fill the gap.

Yes, old age is unpleasant to see and to experience. I remember — it seems a very few years ago — dealing with the final illness and death of my own parents. I know something of what my children feel, but they don't know anything about how I feel. All infants are incontinent and given to crying at night. Nevertheless, I found mine charming, and they will have, now, to take me as they find me.

I ramble, I reminisce, I get lost on familiar roads or start out to do an errand and can't remember what it was. Good people are sorry for me, and bad people take advantage of me. But nobody respects the wisdom I may or may not have acquired in 80 years of living.

I can't pick up a paper or magazine without reading how expensive and burdensome it is to maintain us. Yet I am told that the living will I have signed asking to be allowed to die in the course of nature is probably unenforceable. The models I am expected to emulate are desiccated copies of youth. Even Ronald Reagan tries, no longer very successfully, to look and act like the man he was 30 years ago.

The retirement community in which I live can be represented as the Bastille at the time of the French Revolution, a 20th-century Purgatory, a party from which the unwillingly lingering guest can't get away and the host must continue to go through the motions of hospitality. We have come together here to die.

About us people face death or disability or the loss of a mate with courage and good humor; many others are querulous or frightened. We are not encouraged to think or talk about the mysteries of life that have brought us from helpless infancy to helpless old age. Such thoughts, like any speculations about an afterlife, are gloomy and depressing; we are supposed to knit, play golf or bingo, watch television, enjoy life.

A tidy little blue card on the bulletin board announces death in our community. "We regret to announce the death of . . . " and a name is typed in. This is a proper social lie; they don't regret it at all; it frees another bed in the overcrowded infirmary.

Who are we? Why are we here? Where did we come from? Where are we going? These are questions to be threshed out in college dormitories by youths who think they will never die, not to be revived in our lounges or day rooms.

ANNA MARY WELLS
Hightstown, N.J.

In this poignant self-disclosure, the writer seems to ask for an accessible language in which to express appreciation for herself and others, for the immediate situation and the wider world, indeed for all of life at whatever age and for the forming, reforming, and transforming mystery at its center.

We intend to share in this book our own and others' stories of appreciation in an attempt to alter the painful dissonance you may feel between who you are and the time and place in which you have to live out your everyday existence. We direct its insights and findings to anyone who wants to give a new impetus to his or her life. It may be of particular interest to counselors, educators, spiritual directors, or therapists who hope to help others find more happiness and harmony wherever life brings them.

The book is not intended for people in need of professional help due to severe episodic or chronic depression. We believe it can address and suggest ways to overcome the ordinary low moments we all go through. It can also complement pretranscendent or gnostic counseling for those who have found or are still seeking help on this level of life. It is our hope that professionals in many branches of therapy, including what I initiated as transcendent or transtherapy, will profit from knowing more about the power of appreciation when people come to them seeking counsel and care.

On a more personal note, we believe that this book will offer you a way to redirect yourself when you feel down, angry, needy, insecure, or disappointed. Its aim is to enable you to clarify for yourself how these feelings point to the depreciative obsessive direction you may have assumed somewhere along the way. Examples and stories will show you how to develop effective tactics of redirection, how to shift as quickly as possible from depreciative to appreciative thoughts, feelings, and moods. We want to help you learn how to turn self-defeating depreciation into praise and appreciation.

# THE POWER OF APPRECIATION

*Adversity*

*is*

*a*

*blessing.*

## Chapter 1

# Becoming Appreciative

**P**eople wonder if there are any tried and true ways to overcome the strains and tensions they feel between themselves and their surroundings. They ask, "How can we regain joy and serenity in our life?" Our answer to this oft-repeated question is based on the conviction that appreciation is the single most important disposition to be cultivated in our life and world today. The power of appreciation helps us to look at the directions for living offered by everyday events, good, bad, and indifferent, in a new way. Are you engaged in some form of therapy, counseling, direction, or self-help at this moment? Or are you simply feeling out of sorts? In either case we believe that the style of reflecting and responding described in this book will enable you to rediscover and retain the happiness all humans seek.

Painful as it is to admit, all of us are somewhat off key at times. For days or months, any one of us can lose the sense of life's meaning and purpose. We can tune out the transformative power embedded in the "givens" with which we have to cope on a daily basis. The statistics are convincing. Every year in the United States alone several thousand teenagers commit suicide. Predictions are that two out of three marriages will end in divorce. Hypertensive illnesses and heart disease are still the number one killers in our country. A high number of people in the helping professions suffer from low-grade depression, if not full-blown burn-out.

Jonas Salk, M.D., developer of the polio vaccine, believes that our society is at a crisis stage. There is danger in this, to be sure, but, believing as he does in evolutionary transcendence, he also holds that in such crises human beings manage to produce the knowledge and wisdom necessary to help them choose the most advantageous — and we would say the most appreciative — path.

The fact is, we feel better, more effective, and at home in demanding situations, if we practice the power of appreciation. We can refuse or accept the challenge to improve ourselves whenever, wherever, and however we can. The columnist Ann Landers was asked by someone identified only as a "Fan in Tampa, Florida" to print the following piece, saying she never realized how much she has to be thankful for. The writer calls this reminder "Everyday Thanksgiving."

Even though I clutch my blanket and growl when the alarm rings each morning, thank you, Lord, that I can hear. There are those who are deaf.

Even though I keep my eyes tightly closed against the morning light as long as possible, thank you, Lord, that I can see. There are many who are blind.

Even though I huddle in my bed and put off the effort of rising, thank you, Lord, that I have the strength to rise. There are many who are bedridden.

Even though the first hour of my day is hectic, when socks are lost, toast is burned, tempers are short, thank you, Lord, for my family. There are many who are lonely.

Even though our breakfast table never looks like the pictures in the magazines, and the menu is at times unbalanced, thank you, Lord, for the food we have. There are many who are hungry.

Even though the routine of my job is often monotonous, thank you, Lord, for the opportunity to work. There are many who have no job.

Even though I grumble and bemoan my fate from day to day, and wish my circumstances were not so modest, thank you, Lord, for the gift of life.

Such attunements to what really counts can be powerful on one condition. We need to tap the resources hidden in our past and present experiences if we are to mine the treasures of appreciative living. As we shall see, the power of appreciation dovetails perfectly with classical traditions like the Judeo-Christian that tell us what the good life ought to be. These spoken and written sources of wisdom offer us keys to happiness. We should turn to them every time we seek guidance. How far we come will depend in great measure on the manner in which we received as children the faith and formation traditions that lie at the basis of our spiritual life. If what we learned was open and freeing, we can be sure that growth will occur.

### Moving toward the "More Than"

The power of appreciation starts out from the belief that people are born with the power to search for and choose in life that which appears to give them the most joy and peace, dynamism and delight. Certainly in our pleasure-seeking, functionalistic world this distinctively human capacity to move toward the "more than" (transcendent) remains underdeveloped or overwhelmed by the "less than" (pretranscendent) values that incline us to settle for instant gratification or measurable success only. In neither case can we experience lasting happiness. Pleasure-oriented desires and excessively competitive ambitions, if pursued as ends in themselves, will deflect the aspiration for happiness from its highest goal.

The options offered to us, together with our freely chosen decisions, will color for better or worse the past, current, and future directions of our life. The knack of asking ourselves the proper questions is important. How do we make sense out of the events that shape our day-to-day existence? How can we develop an outlook that will help us to find lasting meaning in life?

One answer is to redirect your feelings, thoughts, and decisions in a way that stimulates appreciation. You will soon discover that life itself, with all its ups and downs, may challenge and surprise you, but never defeat you. Consider this account we received of the death of a friend. While it is unique to the mourner, it reveals the universal sense of loss any lover might feel. This passing weighs heavy on the heart and yet becomes a condition for its uplifting. When the clock of one's own crisis strikes, the hour for believing in the benevolence of a greater mystery is near.

There was no time to mourn. A few short weeks after Paul's death, I discovered a growth that eventually required two surgeries two weeks apart. I had been experiencing minor problems for years and had gone for medical help, but was reassured that everything was fine. This discovery proved otherwise. I couldn't fall asleep that night. It was all too close to Paul's unexpected death. In my mind it had seemed that he would always be there despite my sense of his approaching death. It was just as possible for my own discovery to signal my own death. It wasn't the first time I had to face that possibility, but because I had not even had the time to mourn and move on, but was instantly plunged into my own crisis, everything seemed more "unsettling" than it might have been in other circumstances. I finally somehow let go and handed the entire thing over into God's hands. Then I fell into a deep sleep. God in his goodness ministered to me in an unexpected and incredibly faithful way when I awoke the next morning.

The Lord always seems to "speak" most clearly to me upon awakening. As I awoke that morning and became gradually aware that I was awake, the sense of peace and the clear reassurance that "all would be well" was overwhelming. There was no room for fear. I recognized this peace, for it is a peace that is always with me despite the craziness of my days. Yet it was different in its specificity and in its power. It was a clear, wordless gift of grace. I couldn't even worry. In time this moment would become my only source of reassurance, and it was a reassurance in faith alone.

It took quite awhile to finally have the surgery for three ovarian cysts that had been around for at least two years. My doctor of ten years had carelessly missed them, and he was quite convinced, along with my internist, that they were most probably malignant, as this particular type of a cyst tends to "turn" when untreated early. His panic was frightening. I felt as if I were being pulled down into the vortex of a whirlpool. I couldn't even think. I offered my suffering wordlessly with Jesus. And I remembered his gift of reassurance. On a level deeper than thought, his peace was my refuge. The prayers of those who loved me were so powerful as well. I will never forget how often I would experience waves of strength that were physical as well as spiritual and emotional, and I "knew" that someone was praying for me. I'm sure Paul was one of them.

In the process of becoming appreciative, we tend to develop dispositions and acts that enable us to see the "more than" in the midst of a crisis. We adopt an appreciative view of the world that can bring us new-found happiness, even in the midst of the conflicts and deprivations that are unavoidable in any life worth living.

### Moving Away from the "Less Than"

The word "appreciative" suggests a bent toward that which one finds precious and worth pursuing. It points to a way of directing our thoughts and feelings in a meaningful manner any time we are faced with a difficult person or event.

To opt instead to feel bored, anxious, downhearted, frustrated, angry, resentful, envious, jealous, and joyless does not leave much room for growth. Knowingly or unknowingly you give a direction to your thoughts and emotions that is "less than" appreciative and that is, therefore, depreciative. Whether you realize it or not, you weaken your hidden striving for a happy wholesome life. Pay attention to this depreciative turn of mind and heart. It portends a serious sign of deformation that may tarnish your thoughts and contort your feelings from an early age onward.

You may discover with some self-reflection that this negative stance has become a kind of second nature for you. If this self-defeating disposition is dominant, you may need to consult someone who can help you to take a closer look at yourself. Something needs to be done if you want to correct the detour toward discouragement your life has taken.

Some sound advice would be to develop a kind of inner radar system to pick up the first bleeps of negativity, cynicism, grumbling, or complaining you hear yourself saying outwardly or inwardly. In a relaxed way, try to admit to yourself what is arousing your black mood, bad humor, frustration, or anger. Then do what you can to stop these missiles of madness from reaching the target of your emotional life. Begin to think your way out of and around what is causing this stress to proliferate. Relativize the importance of the complaint. Laugh at the mountain you have made out of the molehill of a little hurt or a moment of misunderstanding. *Consciously practice appreciation.* Try to find what is appreciable even in the most cutting criticism. Listen to what is going on in and around you, but also learn to let go of the hurt. What will this incident matter a million years from now? Refocus on the good, on what makes you happy, as soon as possible. Defocus on what causes you to be unduly stressed or anxious or resentful of others. Be sure not to place the blame for what has happened wholly on yourself or others. Learn to be compassionate and forgiving.

If the depreciative disposition is uprooted as quickly as possible, you may be able to recover lost ground in minimal time. As the unnecessary suffering caused by this misdirection is relieved, you will find yourself becoming effective and joyful once again. *You have what it takes to turn your life around.*

### Tasting the Fruits of Appreciative Living

We are born to be appreciated and to become appreciative. We only need to flow with the grace of gratitude. Once this happens you will delight in your new-found appreciation of self, world, others, and their mysterious source. Appreciation will grow into a warm presence to the gifts in cosmos and creation as expressions of a divine generosity. You will exude care for all that is good.

If you are able on your own or with the help of another to follow this path, you will begin to taste the first fruits of the power of appreciation in a short period of time. Many people report feeling relief slowly and gradually from the oppressive thoughts and feelings that steal their energy and even their will to live. They begin to look at their surroundings with new eyes. Instead of sitting dejected in a corner, they discover how they can make their life useful in any situation.

We do not doubt in the least that you can give a new, more flexible form to your life. The question is: Are you willing to develop a personal program of formation that is consistently faithful to these aims? Resolve here and now to gain insight into what is causing your depreciative feelings. Promise that starting today you will deal with the dissonance that distorts the harmony you seek to restore between yourself and others.

## HOW TO BECOME APPRECIATIVE

1. Look at everyday events in a new way. Tune in to their transforming power.

2. Tap the treasures of appreciative living hidden in your past and present experiences.

3. Guide your aspiration for happiness toward its highest transcendent goal. Seek the "more than." Do not settle for less.

4. Pay attention to any depreciative turn of mind and heart. Redirect it quickly toward what is appreciable.

5. Flow with the grace of gratitude.

6. Exude care for all that is and its benevolent source.

7. Develop a personal program of life formation that will help you to follow the way of appreciation faithfully.

*Failure*
*does not lead*
*to*
*suspension*
*of*
*dedication*
*but*
*to renewed*
*creation.*

*Chapter 2*

# Escaping the Trap
# of Depreciative Thinking

**D**epreciation is a source of unhappiness. It can be more or less severe depending on the circumstances. We can choose to deal with it or we can allow it to overwhelm us. *From the first moment we acknowledge that depreciation is disrupting the way we want to feel, we deflate its dark power.*

Naturalists like Kurt Vonnegut have one word to say about our pathetic penchant to pollute the environment on which we depend for life: *STOP*. He and others sensitive to ecological issues target the out-of-tuneness that exists between us and nature when we forget that the earth is our mother and treat her as if she were a commodity to be used up and thrown away. Once we grasp how out of tune we are with the environment that sustains us, we can become aware of this disposition and stop poisoning the air, water, and soil on which the food chain for all life depends.

We may find effective means on a worldwide scale to relieve the pain of deprived people and to cease building machines of war, as if deterrence alone could solve our problems. We can start dialogues about what human people on the same planet can agree upon as basic to the preservation of their life and world. We can stop being wasteful and destructive. We can start to pray. We can stop thinking we can fix things up by means of our own power alone.

## Correcting Your Course

The "Stop . . . Make a New Start" way may seem at first glance too easy. If you try it out, you may soon find that the symptoms of depreciation diminish and may even disappear totally. We call this technique "appreciative alteration." It helps us more than anything to escape the trap of depreciative thinking. It is fast working. It changes the misdirection of your life in relatively short order. You can learn to use this method on your own or with the help of a counselor or therapist. It can start you on a new path of insight and commitment. You may detect *Just Noticeable Improvements*, or JNIs, on a day-to-day basis. Slowly you may begin to feel inner peace and happiness where before you felt yourself to be only the victim of whatever life held in store.

What can this shift to appreciative thinking do for you? For one thing, you will experience some lifting of the cloud of negativity that veils correct assessment of your situation. Secondly, you will grow in the knowledge of how a wrong self-direction can bring you into conflict with yourself, with God, with others, with your here-and-now surroundings, and with your wider world. Thirdly, you will learn how to distinguish between consonant (in tune) and dissonant (out of tune) feelings and how to appraise your life as a whole in a more realistic fashion. It will then become possible for you to deal more effectively with whatever upsets you. In short, by not giving in to depreciation, you will make room for the power of appreciation. It acts like preventive medicine, enabling you to diminish the pain of dissonance now and over a lifetime.

## Causes of Depreciation

One main cause of this dis-ease is obsession or obsessive life directives: "Do this, don't do that, go here, don't go there . . . " Such rapid-fire demands evoke a variety of willful and tense emotions. You feel confused, split up, out of sorts. Such obsessions may embed themselves in the autonomous nervous system, that part of our biological make-up that causes us to react rather than to respond to events as they happen. As long as you are not aware of these hidden obsessions, you have little or no control over them. They trigger the depreciative thoughts that lead to depressing feelings. Appreciative thinking alters the process. You bring what is troubling you to thoughtful scrutiny and relaxed testing. You stop triggering negativity by choosing to deplete obsessive directives of their power over you. The shift to appreciation can thus begin to halt the hurt from which you have suffered for many years.

Once you escape the trap of depreciative thinking, you learn to appreciate yourself as an effective, free participant in a world that challenges your creativity, appeals to your courage, and invites the continual exercise of your competence. You enjoy a new lease on life.

## Opting for Appreciation

Your field of life never stays the same. You change inwardly and outwardly from birth to death. People come and go, relationships fulfill and disappoint. Some evoke crises; others instill calm. You may feel as if these crises are only dangers to be avoided, but this is not the whole story. In the Japanese, Chinese, and Korean languages, there is a double character for the word "crisis." One means *danger*, the other *opportunity*. Appreciative thinking enables you to see the crises that emerge in your everyday life not as obstacles leading to defeat but as opportunities offering new directions by which to reshape your dreams.

The power of appreciation gives you the practical means you need to make the best of an always somewhat bad deal. Life is never a rose garden free of thorns. Anyone who plants seeds knows that weeds spring up beside the flowers. Our approach seeks to convince you that the power of appreciation rests within you. You can make this power work for you in any crisis. It challenges you to show courage, candor, and conviction instead of complaining, denying the good things in your life, and losing faith.

Every decision you make is shaped by values or directives embedded in the appreciative or depreciative dispositions you favor. Unwittingly, you may have disposed yourself to look at people, events, and things with fear or suspicion. The kind of inner talk you indulge in tends to be more destructive than constructive.

You begin to repeat the laundry list of your depreciations as if they were second nature.

Recall how you felt the last time someone criticized you. You may have fallen into the trap of saying to yourself, "This proves that I am no good. I hate her for reminding me of my worthlessness. Mean remarks like this make life miserable for me. I despise myself more and more."

These automatic negative appraisals form bad thoughts that lead to worse feelings. Attached to them is a high price, the cost of a life lacking in light-heartedness and inner harmony.

The same scene could have been played out much differently. Had you chosen to handle the criticism more appreciatively, you could have said, "Maybe there is something to what I heard. Perhaps I need to think more about why I upset people. This criticism may help me to be more effective and pleasant when I work or talk with others. I am strong and wise enough to bear with the unpleasant side of these remarks. I can profit from the grain of truth in every criticism. I can gain a handle on how people see me, rightly or wrongly." This appreciative response is not about the critique itself but about the way in which you handle it.

You may be disposed from childhood on to see life as filled with opportunities. Or this outlook may be the result of long struggle and practice. Whatever the case may be, this disposition will not take away the first sting of criticism of the way you look, say, or do things. However, it will prevent longer lasting anger and hate, rejection of self and others, or a despisal of life as a whole. The point is this: a momentary sting ought not to mushroom into an overwhelmingly depreciative response to reality.

### Dampening the Fires of Depreciation

When you do feel more dissonant than consonant, more out of tune than in tune, your feelings may be fueled by the pervasive fire of depreciation. Before you know it, you will begin to see yourself and your whole field of life in ways that sap energy, joy, and enthusiasm. Your imagination will be colored by somber hues. You believe that things really are miserable. More often than not what you imagine comes to pass.

Depreciative feelings affect our memory, imagination, and anticipation. They direct us to tell ourselves that life as we know it always has been and always will be a disappointment.

For example, in remembering what happened to you in childhood, you may see only the hurtful things you had to endure. As you try to anticipate what awaits you in years to come, you foresee only further anguish lurking in every corner. This view creates a climate of despondency, dampening your ability to imagine another outcome. The feeling that nothing is right in your life is irrational and unrealistic, but to you it seems reasonable. Your pattern of obsessive directives, that inner whining voice that won't be still, assures you that things can go no other way.

Such one-sidedness always leads to some distortion of reality. It deforms and twists our mind to think only despondently. That is why we must learn to spot coercive demands and directives at once and alter their course. As we apply the "Stop...Make a New Start" way we become aware of the unnecessary suffering, the exhaustion of energy, caused by such things as discouraging memory flashbacks. Deepen in yourself the desire to be free from this pain. Begin to see that you must put the past to rest. Get in tune with your present-day reality. Face the future with hope.

The moment you start out on the journey of transformation, you begin to feel better. Already your decision to engage in a process of reformation will lift your spirits. This appreciative approach is not a panacea. What it offers is a way gradually to attain relief from the litany of depreciations that make life dissonant.

If you persevere in the exercise of the power of appreciation, you can begin, with the help of grace, to taste the fruits of transformation.

### Convincing Examples of Appreciative Living

According to *On the Beam*, the newsletter of New Horizons for Learning, Winter 1991, David Cooperrider and his co-workers at Case Western Reserve University have developed a simple approach to maintaining the health of any organization. They describe this approach as AP, or the "appreciative process." Business consultants G. Bushe and T. Pitman give us the two key elements of AP and how it can be used. The first, identified as "stalking the flow," calls for paying attention to what is going well in a company, rather than focusing on what is going wrong. The aim here is to search for instances of people doing good work or processes that are succeeding. What one "stalks" are not necessarily highly visible improvements but subtle examples of success. The better one understands the "flow," the easier it is to enter into it rather than to resist it.

These consultants know from experience that searching for the positive makes a person popular with co-workers and creates an atmosphere for the second phase of AP, and that is "amplifying through fanning." This means that once the flow is found, one can try to build "a small fire into a big blaze" through praise, blessing, and asking for more creative output. Top managers learn to use AP to improve the flow and to inspire and ease tension on many levels. AP has proven to be most effective when teams devoted to "stalking and fanning" are made up of members from both inside and outside an organization. In all cases the key to AP, researchers and consultants agree, is its encouragement of idea-sharing and risk-taking.

Or take the work of several researchers at the University of Washington and at the Harvard Medical School who are studying the "lapses" typical of a variety of addictions. They insist that lapses ought not to be seen as sources of discouragement but as occasions for learning what went wrong. A lapse is not a relapse. It is a slip. One can appreciate it as such and then muster the courage to start again without making the same mistake.

According to G. Alan Marlatt, a psychologist who is an expert on breaking habits like smoking, "The successful quitters focused on what they might have done differently rather than on thoughts like, 'This just proves I'm addicted to nicotine.'" In a report printed in the *Charleston Gazette* of January 1989, he observed also that those who returned to smoking did not look on the "slip" as a mistake they needn't repeat. Instead they felt only guilty. They blamed prevention programs or the stressful situation for the relapse. They saw it as due to something in themselves they could not change, like a lack of will power. Other types shrugged off the slip as human. They believed that recovering from a lapse would be for them a source of confidence. The formula Marlatt offers to encourage people who want to change is in its own way an appreciative process:

1. Treat the slip as an emergency requiring immediate action.

2. Remember that a slip is not a relapse.

3. Renew your commitment.

4. Review the actions that led to the lapse so you won't repeat them.

5. Make an immediate plan for recovery.

6. Ask someone for help.

Decisive for recovery is a real commitment to do what you can to foster your own change for the better. This course of action, once begun, is never finished. You can always find in yourself new patterns of depreciative thinking that you have to overcome. At times you will fall back into the old ways you have tried to change. You must trust then, as never before, that you can regain your ground and go forward. Lesser obsessions may take the place of the stronger ones you discarded. Subject these to vigilance of mind and heart. They will not deform your life as much as those that used to distort your outlook.

Disclosing and transcending dissonant obsessions signal a steady commitment to transformation — a graced effort we should expect to pursue until our final hour. Our daily field of life will always be loaded with nagging tensions. We cannot hope to eliminate these totally, but we can learn to avoid them or at least to live with them in ways that are less disturbing.

## HOW TO ESCAPE THE TRAP
## OF DEPRECIATIVE THINKING

1. **Deflate the power of depreciation from the first moment you detect it and make an appreciative change.**

2. **Be grateful for *Just Noticeable Improvements* (JNIs) in your depreciative patterns of behavior.**

3. **Temper the compelling power of obsessive directives.**

4. **See every obstacle you encounter as a potential formation opportunity.**

5. If you suffer a relapse, regain your appreciative composure and recommit yourself to transformation.

6. Make the shift to appreciative thinking one of your main goals over a lifetime of trying.

*My grasp*
*of reality*
*as emerging*
*from*
*its*
*deepest ground*
*pierces*
*through the darkness*
*with*
*unexpected*
*intensity.*

## Chapter 3

# Taking the Leap of Faith

**D**ispositions like gratitude and ingratitude affect for better or worse our moods, thoughts, and feelings. Whether we are characteristically upbeat or depressed will be recorded like music tracks on tape in our memory, imagination, and anticipation. Freedom of choice, actions and reactions, physical health, and the ability to recover from disease are barometers of our basic outlook on life. No one can feel happy in the grip of depreciative life directives. These are by definition at odds with our deepest call to joy. They demean us and all those around us.

In a striking and still controversial study at Harvard, psychologist David McClelland showed students a film of Mother Teresa, an embodiment of altruism, working among Calcutta's sick and poor. Tests revealed in those who watched an increase in Immunoglobulin A, an antibody that helps to defend the body against respiratory infections. Even some students who said they didn't like the nun showed the enhanced immune response. Researchers aren't certain what the findings mean, but they hint at a link between altruism and immunity. Whatever conclusions the experiment comes to, it does seem to suggest that our biogenetic make-up "recognizes" what is truly appreciable and responds positively, even if our functional-rational minds tell us the opposite.

## False Starts and Failed Expectations

A first step toward overcoming obstacles like joylessness is to be aware of what you are thinking and to acknowledge how you are feeling. Admit your loss of spark, the numbness and powerlessness you feel in regard to simple, everyday living. Behind such emotions there usually lurk what we call "obsessive happiness directives," or OHDs. These are rooted in the expectations people have of what would or could make them happy. Everyone strives for happiness. How we try to satisfy this desire may be more or less realistic.

When an acquaintance of ours remarried, it was clear that her daughter had made up her mind to despise her stepfather. She became obsessed by the idea that he could never replace her real father. She ignored and defied him until she herself had to cope with a crisis that made her feel helpless, lonely, in search of a new outlook on life. Only then did she realize that her stepfather had been there to support her all along. He was the person, not her biological father, who showed her sympathy and love. Her whole outlook began to change when she stopped obsessing about how wonderful her life would be if her "real" father had never left her and her mother. She was able to see that it was really her stepfather who wanted her to be happy and who showed her the kind of love that changed her life for the better.

Many of our best attempts to find happiness are self-defeating. To live for pleasure-seeking or money-making only cannot guarantee peace and joy. The classic film *Citizen Kane* is a good illustration of the illusory nature of certain so-called guarantors of happiness. Kane had everything money could buy, but at the end of his life the only thing that had any meaning for him was the little sled he used as a child, the toy he called his "Rosebud." He died in despair with this sole word on his lips.

Each dimension of our life has its own set of dynamic strivings and dispositions. Our vital "I" enjoys physical gratification; our functional "I," fulfillment of ambitions, job security, and satisfaction. Yet our deepest transcendent "I" cannot find lasting contentment in these lower dispositions, stimulating and ambitious as they may be.

People in a time of war may experience a shocking loss of everyday sources of security, of food, clothing, and shelter. Conditions on which they had counted for sustenance disintegrate like ashes from spent logs. They no longer enjoy the conviviality and compatibility to which they have grown accustomed. They may be obsessed by an urge to equate restoration of their former lifestyle with total happiness. The exaggeration of the nostalgic memory of the good things of the past may wipe out any other avenue to peace. Those who fail to appreciate a higher dimension of life may grow more and more disgruntled. They do not even try to see a ray of hope in a situation that appears at first glance to be hopeless. They are so stuck in the harshness of their present story that they cannot see any opportunity for transformation.

To equate your aspiration for happiness with the gratification of vital needs only leads also to disappointment. Of course, such vital needs as those for food, clothing, and shelter must be met. This is a matter of good judgment and justice. Still their fulfillment should not be seen as the ultimate and only path to happiness. It cannot give form to the strength of heart you need to survive suffering and deprivation.

By yielding to the obsessive directives linked only with the functional realm of your life, you might wrongly conclude that only the satisfaction of being, for example, a manager, performer, writer, speaker, administrator, teacher, or whatever could lead to happiness. Paradoxically, the inability to bear the loss of functional power and control leads only to more unhappiness. During the Great Depression in America, only those willing to let go of their obsessive and exclusive happiness directives could be saved from despair and suicide.

## Being Committed to Live Appreciatively

What enables some and not others to rise above the limiting notions that breed the illusion that happiness can only be found in vital pleasure or functional control? The answer depends on whether or not one can affirm belief in a beneficial mystery of formation that embraces human life lovingly. Can you accept the challenge to see any situation as an occasion to seek further growth? to become fully alive as a spiritual person?

Being committed to the power of appreciation is the essential step one must take. The dynamic to live appreciatively grows in some cases from a seed of self-surrender to an expansive exercise of universal love. Good examples of this "leap of faith" can be seen in the war diaries and writings of Anne Frank, Edith Stein, Corrie ten Boom, Etty Hillesum, and Dietrich Bonhoeffer. By continuing to exercise faith, hope, and love in the midst of doubt, despair, and hatred, there grew in them the will to do something good despite the debilitating circumstances of their captivity. They supported efforts to free people in prison, to save the lives of those facing arrest, to find food for those who were hungry. Some joined the resistance itself. Others exposed the evil of injustice. All prayed. Whatever their role or call might be, it was clear that the restoration of their potency for love and labor depended on their growth in appreciation.

### Being Aware of the Temptation to Shun Thanks

People seeking to restore their trust and confidence in crisis situations will find that the road is not easy. Especially in times of uncertainty, one has to keep vigilant. Old habits are hard to break. At any moment we can fall under the tyranny of depreciative dispositions engraved, as it were, on the edges of our heart and mind.

At the first sign of giving up, we need to remind ourselves on the spot how a particular fixation of ours leads to needless suffering. Depreciative directives are always accompanied by feelings of frustration and discouraging memory flashbacks.

Every time we are disappointed in our expectations, it may feel as if we have been hit by lightning. The depreciative potency then triggers into an "on" position. You do not like yourself or anyone else. You lose your capacity to keep courage in always limited situations. You feel completely out of control. Life becomes sheer misery.

To resist the temptation to turn "thanks" into "no thanks," you must become aware that depreciative thoughts are the breeding ground of self-defeating feelings. You will find through experience that the possibility for happiness does not depend on attaining what you had sought as the ultimate and only way to it. Fixed expectations of this sort do not guarantee the peace and joy for which you so earnestly long. Disappointment erodes your false confidence. It makes you doubt that you can find happiness. The more despondent thoughts flood your mind, the more you feel trapped in the dead-end streets of self-pity, deception, and defeat.

Delusions of this sort fail to deliver the happy life they promise. Unfortunately, depreciative trains of thought may have become so much a second nature that you are not aware of their destructive power. You only experience the murky feelings left in their wake. You fail to examine and change the thankless thoughts that provoke and accompany these feelings. You underestimate the power of the obsessive happiness directives at the root of your despondency. You only know that your zest for life, your capacity for love and creative labor, are rapidly eroding.

## Exercising Appreciative Appraisal

Every time you feel depreciative and out of tune with your self and your surroundings, try to find the thought that gripped your mind before or after you felt frustrated and defeated. Try to link this thought with an underlying illusory happiness directive flowing from one or the other lower dimension of your life. Ask yourself if you are seeking happiness only in social acceptance and security, only in vital gratification or the satisfaction of power, control, success, and ambition. Then try reasonably to assess these fixations. Recall how much anxiety, anger, loss of energy, suspicion, envy, jealousy, and frustration you have suffered for years because of them.

What else has this self-defeating path bred but more unhappiness? Think about the harm these tense, repeated battles for possessions, pleasures, and powers as guarantors of happiness, have done to your health. No matter how much you thought you had succeeded in this quest, you were never at peace. You were afraid to lose what you had gained. In a sober moment of truth, you may ask, "Can this be the way to lasting happiness?" You may admit once and for all that it does not work. Now try to change the life directives to which you had clung. Turn them into reasonable appreciations of the limited security, pleasure, and satisfaction any lower dimension of life can bring. Do not allow them to become an obsession that controls you.

## Handling Obsessive Happiness Directives

OHDs are the culprits behind your thoughts of failure and disappointment. By now they may have become such a part of your life that your reaction to them is predictable. They are like automatic pilots. Once set, they run their course. You do not have to exercise much effort to start the whole process of pursuing pleasure and satisfaction as ultimate all over again. Just as surely, you will feel let down by ensuing frustrations. By learning to redirect these urgings, by appraising them anew, you can prevent repeated falls from what you imagined to be the peak of happiness.

Handling such tyrannical directives wisely calls for appreciative appraisal. Once you have gained this attitude, appreciation may occur as rapidly as the blinking of an eye. It happens so fast that you may not be aware of its effective power. Once an event, person, or thing triggers OHDs, these demand quick, careful appraisal. Is the excitement you feel genuine or is it based on false expectations? A high pitch of enthusiasm may stimulate action or reaction, but can it last? Once you come down from the mountaintop of elation, are you ready to cope with reality in all its harshness?

Even if you got something of what you were striving for ardently, peace of mind may elude you. In spite of your excitement, you begin to fear you may lose what you have gained. You secretly wonder when you will be let down once again. Depreciative flashbacks tempt you to give in to the downside. Renounce them immediately. Replace them with what we call "appreciative imaginative prospects." For example, someone whose opinion you value says, "Your hair is a mess." You flashback instantly to a self-depreciating feeling. "I hate my hair." Renounce this thought as quickly as you can. Replace it with the prospect, "Great reminder! I'll make that beauty parlor appointment I've been putting off for weeks." This repeated exercise will free you slowly but surely from the depreciative power of self-defeating memories.

When your appraisal is free and realistic, not compulsive and inflated, it will reflect what is really happening in a relationship or in a situation. Liberated appraisal results in realistic feelings of what it is like to gain and lose security, to enjoy and miss pleasant sensations, to assume or relinquish control. This sense of what is real may guide you to a source of peace and joy that is not elusive but lasting. The human spirit rises to meet the stars in the midst of unavoidable adversity.

We seek a more profound meaning of our pain. This appreciative stance will not remove scars, but it will help us to live with adversity in a dignified way. The power of appreciation is rooted in faith, hope, and love in a Higher Power, who empowers us to accept suffering as a path to graced transformation. By contrast, obsessive happiness directives and the distortions of reality that flow from them are deformative. Our fixations on substitutes for true happiness destroy our attunement to life as it is. We should no longer allow our energy to be absorbed by futile pursuits of what in the end disappoints us. This locked up energy has to be set free by the power of expanding appreciation if we are to remain faithful to our deepest call to selfhood in the Sacred.

Spot and defuse your OHDs, never believing that you are beyond the pale of transformation. Do not give in to the irrational spin that perpetuates a despondent life.

Victims of OHDs may become masters of illusion. They possess the uncanny capacity to believe and to convince others that what is passing is really lasting. The German philosopher Josef Pieper writes insightfully about this deception.

> ...both manifestations...the systematic establishment of the work ideal as absolute and the degeneration of the lustful eye — surround themselves with the immense effort of a forced optimism, of a radiating trust in life, of a noisily proclaimed "progress." Everyone knows that belief in progress is declared a social duty in the world of nothing but work. It is also known that *keep happy* and *happy end* belong from the start to the basic elements of this world of illusions, in which the greedy eye has created for itself a replacement for the "fullness of life."

Appreciative, realistic appraisal enables us to transcend these self-deceptions. It helps us to unmask tyrannical, depreciative thoughts, feelings, and happiness directives. It reveals how unwise it is ever to rely on them.

## HOW TO TAKE THE LEAP OF FAITH

1. Do not let any expectation of happiness obsess you or lead to needless suffering.

2. Do not equate your aspiration for happiness with the gratification of vital needs or the satisfaction of functional ambitions alone.

3. Examine and change the depreciative thoughts that evoke despondency.

4. Appraise every OHD and renounce its illusory promises.

5. Relativize the impact of OHDs on your life and reappreciate the realistic good at hand.

6. Believe in the beneficial mystery of formation that embraces human life lovingly.

*Making*

*the*

*best*

*of an*

*apparently*

*bad*

*situation*

*can be*

*a*

*sign*

*of creativity.*

## Chapter 4

# Pursuing Paths
# of Transcendent Transformation

To pursue a transcendent horizon means that you no longer allow your obsessive happiness directives to call the shots in your life; you rise above them. Our lower illusions of fulfillment evoke attachments to the idols of social security, vital pleasure, and functional satisfaction *as if these were ultimate*. The illusion that the human longing for peace, wholeness, and happiness will be satisfied *if only* these demands can be met tightens its grip. Fulfillment of these strivings may yield the dubious rewards of popularity, gratification, and success, but not real happiness.

The lower, or pretranscendent, dimensions of your life ought to be the servants, not the masters, of your highest, or transcendent, dimension. They cannot take the place of the "more than" nor can they, by themselves alone, radiate light into the shadowy corners of the limits of any human life. As servants, these lower dimensions are indispensable; as masters, they spell disaster. They are meant to facilitate the unique unfolding of our life, not to dominate it.

The transcendent dimension holds the highest and deepest dynamic of human existence. To the degree that our existence is in tune with our God-given essence, our life call, and the transcendent tradition to which we are committed, we will be able to live as distinctively human or spiritual persons. This inmost original call, which directs our day-by-day development in time and space, is that of us which emerges from and returns to the radical mystery at the root of life's formation.

We are called to grow in consonance with the mystery over a lifetime of trial and error. What causes trouble is the fact that our life has to unfold in a world inundated with illusions about how to find the happiness we innately crave.

To embody our deepest calling in a complex world, we need to cultivate the social, vital, and functional powers that will enable us to interact effectively with the situations in which we find ourselves. It is our responsibility to develop these lower dimensions as fully as possible. Not to do so is to risk living in an elusive cloud of otherworldly piety.

The secret of success, spiritually speaking, is to welcome these securities, pleasures, and satisfactions not as sources of ultimate happiness but as gifts of the forming mystery reflected in all dimensions of human life.

Illusion is inevitable if we mistake what is passing for *the* exclusive path to happiness. Then it might be our fate to become anxious pawns on the chessboard of life, adventurers caught on a roller coaster ride of ups and downs, pleasures and disappointments, successes and failures. No matter how much income, status, popularity, and success we might amass, it would never be enough to guarantee the enduring peace that surpasses the here-today, gone-tomorrow gratifications of the lower dimensions of life.

As you begin to excel in the art and discipline of appreciative, transcendent living, you need not fear that you will have to leave behind the pretranscendent dimensions of your life. They are and remain indispensable. They are bridges to the effective form you must give to your day-to-day existence in the world. They are channels of communication for your unique gifts and talents. The sociohistorical, vital, and functional dimensions enable you to radiate into your surroundings the refined wisdom of a transformed heart and mind.

### Living in Faithfulness to Transcendent Directives

In this chapter we want to take a closer look at how the dimensions of our life influence our daily strivings. How do they offer us directives for appraisal? What do we make of the countless moments of ordinary seeing and doing, of apprehending challenges and acting decisively? Do we have to think about these transcendent and pretranscendent directives every time we have to make a decision pertinent to daily living? Doesn't that seem impossible?

We must remember first of all that the forming mystery gifted us with a marvelous repository for the directives that guide our daily round of reflection and action. Our formative mind not only stores up, it also implements spontaneously memories of appreciative or depreciative dispositions and acts. It functions as a built-in process center in our brain and nervous system. It enables us to make lightning-speed appraisals and decisions without undue pressure.

We can compare what we mean with the automatic pilot of an airplane. This is the mechanism that provides the crew with the data and directions they need to chart the course they must fly to reach their destination. Once in place, this mechanism can almost guide the plane by itself. It executes automatically the directives inserted by the crew in reaction to changing situations.

There is a comparable inner automatic process center programmed into the airplane of daily life. We have fed various sets of directives — like tapes — into the auto-pilot of our brain. Any situation we meet triggers the feelings, excitements, apprehensions, appraisals, and patterns of action and reaction we have inserted. Because of steady repetition, the process is initially difficult to interrupt once the inserted tape winds out its emotional patterns or responses.

### Properly Programming Pretranscendent Directives

Automatic patterns hooked into our nervous system may contain compelling directives of an obsessive nature driving us to pursue false paths to happiness. These are difficult to remove from the system. Any attempt to "change the tape" always causes psychological or physical withdrawal symptoms. During "reprogramming" we are likely to feel devastated on the one hand, secretly elated on the other.

People who live mainly on the pretranscendent level can

expect their autonomous nervous system to be programmed mainly by the socio-vital-functional facets of life. The insertion of automatic fulfillment directives by the three lower dimensions of life into one's "program" may or may not be in tune with one's original call to live in faithfulness to one's own giftedness.

This higher light is obscured by an intervening form that behaves as if it were the founding form of our life itself. This is identified in the van Kaamian theory of personality as the pride form. It is an autarchic counterfeit form that thrives on the illusion that one can operate by one's own power alone without any sense of ultimate dependency on the divine forming mystery.

The pride form silences our call to transformation by a Higher Power. It convinces us of our own superiority and self-sufficiency. This self-obsession and the directives it generates veil our true transcendent calling. The spurious quasi-foundational form of life drives us to put all our longings for peace and joy into an effort to program and adhere exclusively to the directives issued by the three main pretranscendent dimensions of life. Instead of their being the servants of the transcendent, the socio-vital-functional dimensions become its masters. They usurp, as would a conquering tribe, our access to the land of likeness to the transcendent mystery that carries us.

We all suffer from this fundamental perversion. It gives rise to dissonance. It distorts our apprehensions and appraisals of reality. Such malformation saps our energy. It drains away the wisdom of living. It hinders our ability to grow in loving consonance with our deepest self, with others, with the world, and, above all, with the forming mystery embracing us continuously. Our vulnerability is so great that we cannot rise above it without the grace of transformation.

### Relying on Grace to Guide Us

What does grace mean in this regard? Many minds have addressed this question from the viewpoint of their faith traditions. Our invitation to practice the power of appreciation is not meant for one faith group alone but for people of all creeds who aspire after liberation from an absolute dominance by the three lower dimensions of life. The sheer human longing for peace and joy goes beyond the capacity of any pretranscendent dimension to grant total fulfillment. Yet, in the quest for consonance, we cannot destroy or ignore the unique place and function of also these dimensions in the splendid mosaic of transcendent living.

A simple way to appreciate the wonder and mystery of grace is to ponder the origin of the word. It comes from the Greek *charis*, meaning benevolence shown by the "gods" toward the human race. It is a gift we cannot control or compel. It comes down to us from the goodness of the divine mystery itself. Grace means more than such gifts of nature as the blessing of bodily health; the sharpness of a sound mind; the comfort of food, clothing, and shelter; the power of self-realization. These gifts do not exclude grace. Grace transforms and deepens them while surpassing all human powers and claims. Grace is thus the indispensable means by which we are able to transform our pretranscendent life from the illusion of mastery to the freeing posture of servanthood of what transcends yet lovingly embraces and penetrates us.

The essence of grace resides in its gratuity. Its reception presupposes that we acknowledge, at least implicitly, that life cannot be transformed without the help of a power greater than ourselves. An expression of this truth can be found in the twelve-step program of Alcoholics Anonymous. An AA member knows that he or she cannot be accepted into a group and be brought to a new starting point without admitting that it is impossible to grow beyond this addiction without explicit reliance on a Higher Power.

All alcoholics, no matter their ideological or religious background or affiliation, must admit, according to Step One, that they are powerless over alcohol, that their lives have become unmanageable. Even this honesty is not enough. They must come to believe in Step Two that only a Power greater than they themselves can enable them to cope with their addiction. Then in Step Three they make a decision to turn their will and their lives over to the care of God as they understand God to be. Recovering alcoholics know from experience the amazing grace of a forming mystery that can transform an addicted life into one replete with renewed hope and courage.

## Recovering from Lower Dimensional Addiction

While you may not suffer from the disease of alcoholism, you may be encapsulated in a similar pretranscendent prison. The effects show up in your autonomous nervous system. The directives that give form to your life compel you to crave more material security, pleasure, satisfaction, status, control, possession, and power. You may deny your attachment, but the fact is that it drives you daily. The socio-vital-functional structure of these lower dimensions shapes corresponding directives; it devises idolatrous attachments under the dominance of the pride form of life.

As long as you feel that the path to a happy life can be found by adhering to such dispositions alone, your life will be vulnerable to depreciation, depression, and subtle or felt despair. Sooner or later you will experience that there is never enough security, power, and success available to remove all worry from your path. You may enjoy passing moments and periods of happiness, but there soon looms up the threat of losing what you have. You toss and turn over not gaining what you believe will grant you peace. The contentment for which you hope eludes you like a butterfly that escapes the catcher's net. The moment things cease going your way, you feel dissonance, distrust, fear, anger, persecution by others. Narrow self-enclosure in your self-made plans and projects for a happy life excludes consonance with the mystery and its epiphanic appearances in and around you.

## Experiencing Transformation

Grace opens you up to the possibility of transformation. It frees you from anxious self-containment. It changes you without destroying the effectiveness of your pretranscendent capacity to handle the here-and-now situation.

Grace purifies and enhances your socio-vital-functional gifts, making you more sensitive to the people, events, and things around you. Such enlightenment mellows your appraisals. You become more appreciative. Grace diminishes the automatic fear, anger, and tension that are triggered when problems arise or crises explode your illusory peace, which is really complacency.

Without this gentling of mind and heart, your life may accelerate to a hectic pace. You may begin to overeat or be filled with nervous hypertension and other stress-related symptoms, none of which are conducive to a life of consonance.

Grace is that amazing gift of the mystery that empowers you to awaken to the call to consonance, to the "Cs" of candor, congeniality, compatibility, compassion, competence, and courage, even in the midst of trying situations. These appreciative dispositions of the heart take the place of triggered reactions that lead to dissonance, persecution, delusion, uncongeniality, incompatibility, and harshness of heart.

As grace helps you to cut through the wilderness of anxious preoccupations and puts you on the path to transcendence, you will taste the peace and joy that are its fruit and flower. In the measure that you remain depreciative and overly self-reliant, you cannot begin to appreciate yourself, others, life's harrowing and happy events, the cosmos, and the mystery. You will become the inmate of a lower style of life.

Closed in upon yourself, you may become prone to illness, accidents, ulcers, heart trouble, vascular problems, and a host of psychosomatic illnesses. Worse still, you will be unable to let these ailments serve your ascendence through adversity to the stars of appreciative abandonment and affirmation.

## HOW TO PURSUE PATHS
## OF TRANSCENDENT TRANSFORMATION

1. **Make the pretranscendent dimensions of your life servants of the transcendent.**

2. **Grow in consonance with the mystery over a lifetime of trial and error.**

3. **Radiate through your sociohistorical, vital, and functional dimensions the refined wisdom of a transformed heart and mind.**

4. **Reprogram in a transcendent direction compelling directives that drive you to pursue false paths to happiness.**

5. **Keep your pride form in check by recalling your ultimate dependency on the divine forming mystery.**

6. Rely on grace to help you to transform your pretranscendent life from the illusion of mastery to the freeing, humble posture of servanthood.

*To*
*truly*
*transcend*
*a*
*situation*
*I must delve*
*more*
*deeply*
*into it.*

## Chapter 5

# Recognizing Roadblocks
# to Transcendence

We need the grace of transcendence to escape the dead-end streets of dissonance and depreciation. One main hindrance to flowing with grace is the automatic directive of self-protection at any price. This measure is partly instinctual, partly learned from birth through our environment. Mechanisms of fight or flight are often traceable to impulses that were triggered in us as children when anything in our surroundings threatened our security. Anxious directives for self-protection may have become a tyrannical force dominating and deforming us later in life.

Liberation from such reactions is necessary to release the floodgates of transcendent formation. For example, the search for pleasure on the vital level, for gratification through food, drink, sensuality, and sexuality may issue compulsive "orders" to the autonomous nervous system that block the power of appreciative ascendance. By the same token, ambition, manipulation, competition, and control on the functional level, when absolutized and combined with untempered cravings for power and possession, present another formidable roadblock on the path to a peaceful life.

## Relying on the Pride Form

Compulsive directives embedded in the lower dimensions of life are difficult to overcome. This is because they insert compelling "oughts" into the vital and functional dimensions of life in a blind, indiscriminate way.

Our autonomous nervous system is a remarkable gift of the mystery. Its efficiency or deficiency in service of giving consonant, harmonious form to our life depends on the directives we insert into it. These can be rooted in self-centered demands and desires that evolve as outgrowths of our fixation on a self-sufficient form of life. In some sense, all obsessive happiness directives can be traced to such strivings for total self-sufficiency.

Our journey toward transcendence is wholly dependent on our willingness to respond to the invitations of grace to relinquish reliance on our insulated self or pride form alone. Restless clinging to impulsive and compulsive ways of self-protection, vital pleasure, and functional control burrows into our autonomous nervous system like a parasite on an unwary host. Hid by their presence is the sight of the promised land of peace and transcendent appreciation. To grow beyond compulsions that paralyze our spirit, we must transform them.

## Ensnared by Inordinate Attachments

Deep down we are a call to wholeness and holiness. Our original nobility keeps recalling us to itself. In each call to be who we are there resounds the eternal echo of the forming mystery like the soft murmur of the sea caught in a swirled shell left on shore.

Early in life the song of our dignity may be silenced by forces rampant in our profile of sin or our history of deformation. A string of overbearing directives fills our consciousness with claims that betray what we are uniquely called to be. Obsessions stick like barnacles to the ship of life. They slow down our homecoming to the lost harbor of our divine beginnings.

## Liberation through Appreciation

The serenity of a detached heart is not easily attained. Yet every formation event and our response to it can lead us further along the path to appreciative living. We have to allow grace to teach us how to assess even our mistakes as an opportunity for growth.

Singer and artist Tony Bennett made a good point in this regard in an interview published in the February 1992 issue of *Parade Magazine*. Asked if he could live his life over again, would he do anything differently, he replied:

> Whatever I am, I accept it. There are a lot of things I don't know or think I ever will, but I try to sketch and learn as much as I can. I don't regret anything. You see, the great thing about painting is that a lot of paintings don't work, and it dramatizes what happens in life. When you first start painting, and it doesn't work out, you're devastated. But you keep painting. Then you're not bothered by your mistakes. You just say, "The next time will be better." That's what happens in life. That's why I wouldn't change anything. . . . I made mistakes, but those mistakes taught me how to live.

Grace, not your own efforts, will turn your life around too. It will enable you to break loose from the snares of lower living that cause your repeated loss of peace and joy. Before this miracle of transformation occurs, you may have enjoyed brief but passing moments of serenity, effectiveness, right seeing, and prudence. Yet to be disclosed is the depth of your own and others' wisdom, dignity, and creativity. The "new you" grace calls into being will not exclude disturbance and suffering, but it will take away the futile worry that arises from occasional mistakes, errors of judgment, and illusory quests for fulfillment.

An appreciative attitude gives new meaning to setbacks and sorrows. It enables you to cope with rough and smooth spots on the path ahead. You no longer ascribe events that rock your complacency to chance alone. You experience them as challenges drawing you into deeper intimacy with the transforming mystery. You begin to enjoy a new-found peace even when you find yourself once more in a desert of loss and deprivation. You know that nothing can prevent you from finding comfort and strength in your divine source and end. In desolation and consolation, the power of appreciation will keep the flame of a firm and lasting faith burning in the depths of your being.

## Growing in Epiphanic Sensitivity

From the beginning to the end of your journey, transforming grace will alert you to ways in which you may have unwittingly turned aside from epiphanic (God-manifesting) signs and symbols coming from your everyday field of presence and action. Grace will make you see that your lower formation consciousness has been conditioned to look at incoming information in ways that alienate you from the unique dignity of yourself and others.

Overinvolvement in the world dims epiphanic sensitivity. Humility and truth cannot light up in a preoccupied mind and heart. Grace reminds you that you have not been sufficiently vigilant to the dissonance within your own and others' lives. Are we not as people becoming increasingly out-of-tune with the mystery? Do we not all face the threats of nuclear annihilation, ecological disaster, racial and cultural discrimination, social injustice and persecution, the horrors of tribal and national wars, of violent revolutions?

Universal dissonance is at the root of countless causes separating us from each other and from the cosmic epiphanies in and around us. Unless we strive, with the help of grace, to overcome this downspin into selfish isolation, we become vulnerable to the ultimate delusion — that violence, not love, is the normal way human beings inhabit the world. It would seem at this point in history that we have no choice but to grow in epiphanic sensitivity, or sensitivity to the divine call in all things, and to move from alienation to appreciation.

## HOW TO RECOGNIZE ROADBLOCKS
## TO TRANSCENDENCE

1. **Exercise caution in regard to the deforming effects of excessive directives for self-protection rooted in your threatened pride form.**

2. Be responsive to the invitations of grace to go beyond your reliance on your autonomous self alone.

3. Allow grace to teach you how to assess even your mistakes as openings to further growth.

4. Dispel the futile worry that arises from illusory quests for fulfillment.

5. Trust that the power of appreciation will keep the flame of a firm and lasting faith burning within you.

6. Be vigilant to signs and symbols of the Transcendent coming to you from your everyday life.

*We are*
*unwise*
*to*
*throw away*
*the*
*precious*
*pearl*
*because*
*it is offered*
*in an*
*unsightly*
*shell.*

*Chapter 6*

# Moving from Alienation
# to Appreciation

**S**elf-alienation is a sign that we search for happiness by striving futilely to gratify only the desires and ambitions of the pre-transcendent dimensions of our personality. Little wonder we feel frustrated. The unending battle to acquire more things drives us into a spiritual wilderness of competition, envy, worry, and resentment. It gives rise to arrogance, outbursts of highs and lows, false pretenses, disappointments, and despondency.

You may be successful in making money, gaining recognition, getting promotions, and expanding your power base. Sexual conquest, growth in skills and knowledge, the acquisition of degrees, trusteeships, and honorary titles may be "no problem." Yet the more you succeed in these ambitions, the less contented you may feel. Having put your hopes for happiness in such achievements alone, it ought not to surprise you when disappointment nips at your heels. It becomes difficult to suppress the gnawing questions people continue to ask in the consumer society: Is this all there is to life? Are things really more important than spending time together? Is the good life defined by what you own or by who you are?

What gives us pleasure, what we consume or possess, do not in themselves quell the hunger for the "more than." What imprisons us is the anxious claim that this or that *must* be had if we are to be happy. It prevents us from flowing with our transcendence dynamic.

## Signals of Self-Alienation

You may hesitate to let go of obsessive happiness directives because you do not know what will replace them. You are beset by
the fear of failure. You hate the thought that others may outdo
you. Perhaps they will usurp your functional chances of success?
Perhaps they will make fun of you for wasting your time in the
pursuit of life's finer offerings.

You cannot feel appreciative under such pressure. It is under-
standable why you might become angry and alienated. When
someone seems to stand in the way of your bid for control, the
results are predictable. You feel overanxious if what you have
attained seems threatened. Boredom sets in if your dreams of
making it never seem to be fulfilled. No matter how much you
achieve, collect, and indulge in, you still feel unhappy. You worry
about the future. Will you find the means to satisfy the endless
demands of your ambitions?

As time passes and life does not seem to work out the way
you planned, you feel anxious and tense, depressed and burnt
out. Lack of fulfillment after so much effort makes you doubt the
whole meaning of your life thus far. Is existence just a matter of
being born, finding "it," losing "it," and fading away? Your inner
life is in turmoil. That after which you strove so ardently keeps
eluding you.

There is no life that does not have its ups and downs, its peaks
and valleys. The problem is that depreciative living keeps the experience of self-alienation alive. We have no choice but to move
in the direction of appreciation if we want to break the debilitating cycle of being upset by the inevitable losses and gains life
brings. The gifts associated with the pretranscendent dimension
of life are good. In moderation many are attainable, but they do
not in themselves constitute the essence of deeper happiness. As
one wealthy industrialist was purported to have said, "How many
yachts can you water ski behind?"

## Signposts of Appreciation

Traversing the path of transcendence will teach us the way to
overcome alienation from our deepest self. Say your self-image

is that of being an insecure person. You do not like to admit how frightened you feel. You tend to put the blame on something or someone besides yourself. "They did it to me," you say. You tell yourself that impossible people and situations are the causes of your failures. You refuse to listen to your own inner call to freedom from such feelings. Neither high peaks of hope nor low ruts of disappointment account for your alienated condition.

The solution is to do what you can to move toward self-appreciation. The divine forming mystery seeks to deliver you from empty delusions of total control. Letting go may give you a sudden and powerful lift. Living as a servant of the transcendent does not mean that you have to give up whatever you need to hold down a job, begin a family, or build a career. If anything, transformed living increases your energy, heightens your efficiency, deepens your care.

Transformation through appreciation can turn you into a loyal citizen, a dedicated member of the community, a responsible employer or employee. The key to unlocking this power is detachment from unrealistic, self-alienating expectations.

Status, fame, and control are servant sources of formation, not the end of the story. Material things, no matter how many you have, cannot quell the restlessness of your heart. Only deep inner transformation enables you to sense the sacred in everyday surroundings, to abide patiently with what is, to await new disclosures of meaning.

Once you are able to appraise candidly what the mystery asks of you, you may begin to see that daily life itself can become a kind of "director" of your formation. The grace of appreciative living endows you with the wisdom to be present where you are, to live every day as a new find that fosters transformation.

Therefore, you must "change the tape" that aggravates and depletes your energy. Renounce gently yet firmly the dissonant directives and claims that draw you too powerfully. Put away the memories and phantasies that disturb your peace of mind.

Becoming aware of what jars your inner serenity helps you to spot when and how you slip into modes of alienation from your deeper self. Be able to say with humor: "There I go again, playing the same old tape, overconcerned with unimportant things. Let me listen to the invitation of grace and quickly change my tune." Commotions may then become compasses steering you from alienation to appreciation.

### Making a New Start

Begin now to let your divine life call direct you. Erase once and for all the alien life directives that disrupt your ability to flow with grace. Feel the warmth of divine consonance in your deepest center. Peace is no longer a distant goal, a far-off star. It is the sudden and expanding effect of being truly present where you are.

In the light of your new-found freedom, admit how much energy you have lost in the struggle to maintain your depreciative feelings and coercive strivings. Did you not try to manipulate even the people you love, to shape them to fit your projects? Did you not live in the illusion that were you to succeed in this struggle, you would be happy, blissful, unperturbed?

Such grasping for a life of pseudo-peace is as elusive as looking for a pot of gold at the end of a rainbow. No matter how hard you try to make others over, they will resist your best attempts. You will never find contentment on the basis of such false premises.

Willful efforts to push against the pace of grace rather than to flow with its transforming power always end up in some form of alienation. We must learn to find consonance in the midst of dissonance, to appreciate passing moments of peace amid myriad imperfections.

Through the power of appreciation, self-defeating alienation may lose its hold on us. Believe in the promise and possibility of deliverance. Begin the journey from deserts of depreciation to the cool and luminous lands of transcendence awaiting you. Then the mystery that embraces you lovingly will guide you to honest self-examination and the liberation it allows on every level of your life.

### HOW TO MOVE FROM ALIENATION TO APPRECIATION

1.  **Detach yourself daily from lingering attachments to pleasure, power, and possession as ultimate.**

2. Dispel the delusions that prevent you from flowing with your transcendence dynamic.

3. Remind yourself daily that depreciative living makes it difficult, if not impossible, for you to overcome alienation from your deepest self.

4. Listen to your own inner call to freedom from feelings of self-doubt and depreciation, from empty delusions of total control.

5. Live every day as a new find that fosters transformation.

6. Traverse the path of transcendence that guides you to honest self-examination and new expressions of the power of appreciation.

*Life*

*is*

*ebb and flow,*

*joyful and tragic,*

*honest and deluding.*

*Only when*

*we accept*

*this*

*alternation*

*can we rest*

*in the*

*peace*

*that passes*

*understanding.*

## *Chapter 7*

# Seeking Deeper Peace

❖

**E**ncapsulated in a prison of unrealistic desires while holding  the key to freedom is reason enough to feel downhearted. The more we push ourselves and others, the less we see good results. Instead of being content as a matter of course, we experience pockets of peace here and there but relatively little lasting harmony or inner tranquillity. We begin to realize that every attempt we make to attain total happiness cut off from our deeper self and its transcendent source leads to disappointment. Forgetting the "more than" or finding substitutes for it only gives rise to demands for the "less than" that diminish true joy. Deliverance depends on our ability to first detect and then to defuse obstacles to transcendent peace that hinder the very exercise of our power of appreciation.

### False Promises of Fulfillment

As hunting dogs trail the scent of prey, so are we prone to follow the roads of false security, pleasure, satisfaction, and control put forth in a consumer society. The media hail these as trustworthy indicators of what we should own and do to enjoy the good life. The trouble is, no one has ever found ultimate fulfillment in this way. Empires have fallen in the face of such delusion. Flashes of fun, spurts of satiety are enticing, but no lasting peace is possible without steady attunement to the restlessness of our heart for the "more than."

Gnawing desires frequently pose as guides to the dance of life lived abundantly. You may tell yourself many times over: "If I can just become the chairperson of the social club, the leader of the football team, the honor student of the class, the boss of the company, the boyfriend or girlfriend of so-and-so, then I will be happy. If I would earn an academic degree or publish a book that becomes a bestseller, then I would never want anything again."

These aims are not bad in themselves. Dreams can spur us on to use our gifts. Success is stimulating. We like the sweet taste of comfort, the rewards of competence. However, to expect anyone or anything to bring us to the pinnacle of lasting security, satisfaction, and serenity is to miss the mark. It is to betray our call to transcendence.

### Depreciative Effects of Self-Preoccupation

Say you meet a friend with whom you experience instant affinity. You enjoy good times together, everything is going great, but for some reason, after a while, your relationship begins to sour like milk mixed with vinegar. The silences between you are prolonged. Confidential communication all but ceases. Your respect for one another's uniqueness begins to wane. Depreciative emotions overwhelm you. You grudgingly admit that he or she cannot accommodate the expectations triggered by your obsessive happiness directives and programmed into your autonomous nervous system.

The most serious consequence of pretranscendent desires for fulfillment is the depreciative worldview they arouse. This view tempts us to appraise others only as either securing or threatening our well-being. It signals the predominance of self-preoccupation. This fallacious directive inclines us to choose as ultimate what is self-serving. This choice leads in turn to willful, demanding behavior that secretly or overtly evokes resistance. It stimulates counterclaims and demands, envy and abuse. It leaves scars that set you up for more clashes, even with those you love. You become uptight and touchy about everything. You are less able to see what is appreciable in every person. You lose compassion. You feel indifferent to others' suffering.

Unless your attitude changes, depreciation, not peace-loving presence, is bound to guide your appraisal. You begin to see others only as potential threats. You become more tense and aggressive. You place yourself in a fight-or-flight posture. Your heart beats faster. Your power of appreciation grows dim. Your struggle to cope with the imagined threat of others keeps you on the defensive. Your overriding goal of self-protection results in bouts of rage, acrimony, and aggravation. You become irritable and hard to live with whenever things fail to go your way. You feel the slumbering tiger of resentment about to leap any time your anxious self-concern runs into resistance or contradiction.

### Necessity for Reappraisal of Your Worldview

Self-help begins when you take stock of your life. Try to see that no event, person, or thing can pose an ultimate threat to your peace. You are your own worst enemy.

Imagine that someone threatens you by talking behind your back, or making fun of your achievements, or calling you a fake, or turning a department, neighborhood, or even a member of your own family against you.

First ask yourself if you can do something about it. Is it possible to confront the gossiper directly? If so, are you willing to seek a solution as soon as possible or do other factors caution you to wait? In your eagerness to solve the problem do not exhaust your energy by setting up other attachments — now to your very projects of problem solving! Each such attempt blocks appreciative living.

Perhaps at present you cannot do anything about what is annoying you. Relativize its importance. Don't lose your peace. Don't focus on what can go wrong or get worse. Ask for the grace to accept what is happening to you as part of the chain of situations, pleasant and unpleasant, that the mystery allows in your life. Seek for a reasonable way to resolve this passing difficulty. Be ready to let it go. The time may not be right for course correction and reconciliation.

Depreciative emotions, if not inspired by the deeper appreciation they are meant to serve, will drain the energy you need for overcoming greater obstacles to transcendence. Worry diminishes your powers of appraisal. It lessens your ability to apply creative measures to move beyond what seemed to be an insurmountable difficulty.

Worry stirs social, vital, and functional concerns like swirling dust on a country road. It obscures the light of the transcendent. It negates joy. Soon depreciative dispositions and directives encapsulate you in a web of inordinate attachments that retard transition to a higher life.

## Appreciation Leads to Peace

No matter how bad things seem to be, we can take an appreciative stance toward them. We can live in hope-filled abandonment to the mystery. The peace of appreciation lifts us beyond what hassles us emotionally.

The portal to peace in this life is appreciative appraisal. We must continually appraise if we stay faithful to our providential call. This goes before and goes beyond whatever other gifts we may also receive.

To come to consonance means appreciating not only who I am but also what I am called to do in the light of God's design. Placed before each of us is the invitation to believe in the mystery as either caring or indifferent. Our option to believe in God's care has to be renewed daily. It should carry us forward over the course of a lifetime.

Each event in life is a point of departure. We may have to make an appreciative abandonment option in the face of social injustice or other ethical conflicts that challenge us. The question "What must I do?" is not always easy to answer.

For example, as a worker in a company, you may experience unjust labor conditions. You cannot pretend these do not exist or wait for them to disappear magically. You can choose to see what has to be done as a divine challenge and act to improve working conditions. Rather than approaching the adversity by becoming anxious or obsessive, rather than letting animosity overload you with frustration and anger, it is important to remain wisely detached and earnestly attentive. If you are ready to explode at the first provocation, little will be accomplished.

Pretranscendent demands interfere with the task at hand and disrupt our thought process. We have to rise above the pain of personal hurt if we hope to experience equanimity. While remaining gentle, we must firmly protect the rights and needs of ourselves and others.

Countless examples could be given to prove that without the power of appreciation it is impossible to walk this road effectively. Like it or not, most of us at one time or another are trapped in wrong judgments. Fortunately, grace comes to our aid and enables us to remove the barriers blocking obedience to our deepest life call. To be faithful, it is necessary to resist the pull of a depreciative society. Remember, none of us is an isolated entity. We are children of God, called by name, endowed with a unique dignity and destined for glory.

## HOW TO SEEK DEEPER PEACE

1. **Do not program obsessive happiness directives into your autonomous nervous system lest you lose your peace.**

2. **Do not choose as ultimate what is self-serving unless you want to provoke resistance and remain discontented.**

3. **Try to see what is appreciable in every person and situation so as not to lose your patience.**

4. **Try to see that no one but you can pose an ultimate threat to your equanimity.**

5. **Seek creative ways and means to move beyond whatever seems to be an insurmountable difficulty.**

6. **Do not retard your transition to the transcendent by useless worry when you can opt instead to live in appreciative abandonment in spite of your failures.**

*We*

*cannot*

*cease*

*searching for*

*answers,*

*any more than*

*we*

*can*

*stop asking*

*meaningful*

*questions.*

*Chapter 8*

# Detecting Sources of Misdirected Appraisal

**T**he power of appreciation affects all spheres of our life and world. It is the doorway to wisdom. It heightens our awareness of what is precious and praiseworthy within us, others, and nature, within the immediate situation and what lies beyond it. The power of appreciation enables us to go beyond the obsessive dispositions that despoil our chances for a joyful life.

In each situation we must set our priorities wisely. What should I take care of first, what next? For example, one morning you awaken after six hours' sleep and still sense how tired you are. You feel weary around the edges. You are far from feeling rested, and your body tells you that you are still overstressed and tense. This vital warning can either be ignored or taken into account, appraised as meaningful or meaningless, affirmed as requiring a response or denied. Maybe it is time to acknowledge your fatigue, take it easier that day, give yourself the luxury of doing nothing.

To hear what any dimension of life is telling you, you have to listen with loving attention. Assess prudently what is, not what you would like to be. Every time you distort reality, it becomes a source of false direction. These misdirections may manipulate your imagination, lifting you into an "if only . . ." world that makes re-entry into the real one more difficult. Self-inflicted crises and conflicts soon empty your cup of happiness. Before discussing in upcoming chapters further conditions for appreciative living, let us recount ten of the main ways in which people are inclined to ignore or misread the signals for appreciation life sends their way.

## One-sided Appraisal

You may be inclined to appraise your life experiences from the viewpoint of only one or a few events. A pleasant looking girl told us, "I'm ugly because I have a pimple on my nose." An excellent chess player who lost a game after winning many matches mis-directed his appraisal by saying, "Now I'm sure I'm not a good player." A devout lady who was experiencing dryness in prayer complained after a long period of desolation, "God cannot love me. I must be no good at heart. I'm probably doomed."

One-sided appraisal directs you to look only at the part of your life you have depreciated. You need a wider view to focus your attention beyond what you see through this one window. Life is more than a pimple on your nose or a chess match lost. A transcendent choice enables you to reappraise appreciatively every person, event, and thing you encounter in the course of daily life.

Most of the time misguided obsessions hide deep fears. You may be afraid you will feel like a misfit if you lose control. So you tiptoe around life as if it were a mine field. You slink away from people who threaten you. You shudder at the thought of letting go, admitting your vulnerability, trusting the mystery.

Appraisal prompted by fear is likely to be unrealistic. What goes on around us is never totally good or bad. No one's life is absolutely pleasant all of the time nor is it totally lacking in light. If you focus only on what looks bad, you will find it more and more difficult to deal with what is. You will miss many of the most meaningful messages of life. The disconnection between your appraisal and things as they are becomes more obvious. You start to feel increasingly aggravated. Whatever you think, plan, or do fails to match the pattern of the flawless field you imagine.

One-sided appraisal of your life direction is a serious obstacle to the power of appreciation. It inclines you to see everything as good or bad. Shades of less good or less bad do not exist in your mind's eye. You exclude any other meaning. The opposite of this exclusive approach is that of inclusive appraisal of life's direction. The latter takes into account the messages from your world as a whole. You let all of them bear on your appraisal, decision, and action here and now.

### Painting the Entire Field with the Same Dirty Brush

Remember what it was like to paint the walls of an aging shed in the backyard. When your brush got stuck on a dirty spot and you kept on painting, the dirt from that one spot spread out and discolored the rest of the wall.

This is what happens when your appraisal gets glued to an unpleasant experience. You begin to paint your whole life with the "dirt" of one bad thing that happened to you. You tell yourself that this incident is typical of the way things are. You paint your entire past and future with one dirty brush.

A student had bad luck. The teachers in different classes asked her twice in a row questions she could not answer. Her appraisal was, "Teachers are always picking on me!" She started to paint every teacher with the same brush, even though she had to admit, when questioned later, that no teacher had addressed her more than any other student.

The feeling that your field of life has become oppressive is due almost entirely to this besmirching of your experiences with one or a few painful happenings. The depreciations that follow infect subsequent appraisals. You see life as only dreary.

A boy got a bad report card. He feared his parents would berate him. Instead of appraising this as one brief bout with failure, he saw himself as a lasting loser. His mood became so despondent that he tried to kill himself.

A young woman just married had her first fallout with her husband. She ran back to her mother, crying that her marriage was on the rocks.

This kind of distortion of reality acts like a contagious disease. Through contamination, the bad appraisal of something happening in one part of your life spreads out over the whole, clouding past, present, and future. This negating tendency may sooner than later become a lasting disposition, written not only in your conscious mind but embedded also in your autonomic nervous system.

Any time something threatens your "dirty brush" appraisal, depreciative directives begin to unroll in your brain like tapes that won't stop playing. Before you know it, you are aroused by emotions that compel you to fall back into the same bad mood and interpretation. Such feelings, false though they are, are experienced as normal emotions. You fail to see that they are not responses to what is happening in your field of life but reactions to your distorted appraisals. You cannot change these directly. You must get at the fixed ideas behind them. Only by doing so can you begin to reform little by little such erroneous and thankless dispositions.

You must stop the wrong pattern the moment it begins to unroll. Say no to it. Try to disclose the appraisal behind it and examine why it is really a misappraisal. If the distortion is deeply hidden, if you cannot find its cause by yourself, you may have to complement your self-direction by help from a professional.

### Percolating Appraisal

A percolating coffee pot lets hot water soak through the grinds again and again until the water is as dark and flavorful as the original roast. Something similar happens in percolating appraisal. The scalding water of bad feelings soaks so thoroughly into your mood of depreciation that your whole outlook is soon as dark as your moment of disappointment.

A young bride prepares eagerly for her husband's homecoming from work. She puts his slippers by his favorite chair, has a tasteful meal on the stove, readies a drink for them to relax with before dinner. He storms through the door after a busy day, dead tired from talking to demanding clients, irritated by a warning from his boss that layoffs are looming, upset that the paperboy threw the evening news in a wet bush. When he bent down to pick it up, he strained his back. He comes through the door, seemingly oblivious to her careful preparations for his homecoming. She feels let down and won't let go of her disappointment. It percolates with her bad feelings about similar episodes. Soon the whole marriage seems bleak to her. She overlooks the possibility that he had a bad day at the office, making it hard for him to think of anything else. Dwelling on her sense of feeling depreciated conjures up other depressing memories. She does not allow her attention to shift to moments that may give rise to appreciation. Having engaged in selective appraisal, she hinders the ascent to new peaks of peace and joy. The person most harmed by this percolating approach is sadly herself.

## Depreciation of Appreciative Appraisal

If you live in depreciation, you tend to turn every opportunity for appreciation into a new obstacle. You become so accustomed to living a life devoid of bliss that you fail to notice the damage being done to your body, mind, and spirit.

Someone praises you for a good deed you did or for the way you look. The word "praise" is related to the word "appraisal." Honest praise makes you feel good, unless you are obsessed by self-depreciation. Then your immediate retort might be: "They do not really mean it. They only say such things because they feel sorry for me. It's really a trick to get something out of me. I wonder what the hook is. What are they trying to put over on me? After all, I know I'm not that good-looking. This dress is an old rag." Your response is as chilling as a cold shower. The moment the warm water comes on, you turn the tap off until the icy stream chills you to the bone. If you think the opposite every time you hear a compliment, you rob yourself of the chance to feel confirmed by others.

Welcome honest confirmation. It helps you to appreciate yourself in gratefulness to the mystery at the center of your life and world. Grace gives you a beautiful gift: the possibility for true transformation. Grace is the fountainhead of what is best in you. The mystery of divine love is limitless in its appreciation of who you most deeply are. This same mystery moves others to foster your growth. It is at the root of all appreciative relationships. Listen to it with the ears of your heart and soon you will hear the confirmations expressed by others.

Don't reverse honest words of praise offered by well-meaning people. Appreciate yourself and them as gifts of the mystery. Self-affirmation like confirmation by others is a necessary ingredient to living a felicitous life. Whatever else you do, avoid assiduously the trap of reverse appraisal. Recall how much aggravation, loss of energy, bodily weakness, conflict, and pain have been caused by your somber outlook on life.

Becoming aware of your inclination to reverse appreciation is not enough. It is only a first step. It must point the way to an examination of the thoughts that preceded your feelings of suffering and sadness, of guilt and remorse. Now you must try to free yourself from the tyranny of emotions that keep repeating themselves with the same inflexible pattern. If you choose instead of reverse appraisal the way of reforming appraisal, your emotional life will begin to blossom. Your feelings will become vibrant responses, not driven reactions, to the realistic blessings and burdens of every life worth living.

## Logic of Depreciation

Logic is a significant part of the art and discipline of the reasoning process. The mind can use this ability for good or ill. None of us coolly undergoes what happens unexpectantly to us. Disappointment, elation, sorrow, and excitement are emotions that resound in our heart and stimulate our mind. We wonder why such and such a thing happened to us. What does it mean? What can we do about it? Logic gives rules for good reasoning, for clear thinking, but it can become twisted if the process starts out on the wrong foot.

If you are depreciative, if you are convinced that people look down on you, that nobody really likes you, that something bad is going to happen to you, your reasoning, no matter how logical, will be twisted by this false starting point.

Suppose you have spent hours cooking a delicious meal for a family celebration. One of your aunts does not eat much. Maybe she just had a tooth pulled, but you don't know this. You think, "The food must taste terrible. I'm a rotten cook." This way of depreciative reasoning carries so much weight that you do not even bother to check its accuracy.

Suppose it's your birthday. Everyone in the office congratulates you, but your boss fails to remember the date because he is preoccupied with a pressing business problem. You reason falsely, "He does not care about me as a person, only about my ability to perform. He really thinks I'm second rate. I guess I'm lucky to even have a job."

Perhaps your little boy, who is beginning to grow up, does

not want to give you a goodnight kiss. Feeling he is becoming a "man," he shies away from such childish gestures. Your heart sinks as depreciative logic triggers the thought, "My own son doesn't like me anymore. What did I do wrong?" You may respond to this warped reasoning by closing yourself off from him or by responding with angry or whining words. These only serve to create distance and tension where there were none before.

The false logic of depreciation twists your view of the future; it distorts your anticipation of what will happen to you.

A female minister kept telling herself that in the midst of her sermon she would forget what she had prepared; she would be the laughing stock of the congregation. This anticipation belied the truth that she had never once been lost for words in the pulpit. A basketball player explained to a friend why it was logical for him to give up the game: "I am absolutely sure that anything I do will ruin the best chances of my team." His twisted logic expanded a few on-court failures to a feeling of his being hopelessly inadequate. In fact he was a good player, highly appreciated by his coach. Because the coach wanted to keep him for several more seasons he encouraged him to seek counseling.

Perhaps you have found yourself caught in a spin of similar false reasonings. Suppose you send a gift to a friend who is getting married. Apparently she forgets to mail you a thank-you note. You feel a surge of self-depreciation as you tell yourself, "She doesn't even find me important enough to thank me. I better stay away from her in the future. She thinks I'm only a bother anyway."

Such depreciative logic succeeds in making you feel miserable. Soon thereafter your package comes back from the post office with the message that they could not deliver it because you wrote the wrong address. All the churning of your mind, it turns out, was just a lot of convoluted reasoning dictated by your feelings of self-doubt and low-grade depression.

### Increasing and Decreasing Appraisal

A small boy loved to walk around the marketplace near his home. What he enjoyed most was the pitch of the salespeople trying to convince customers to buy their wares. One whom he never forgot was a vendor of binoculars. He told the public: "If you go to the shore, take my binoculars with you. Say you see a wonderful looking girl going for a swim. You look through the magnifying glass. She appears before your eyes in all her beauty. Now say your mean mother-in-law goes to the same shore. You turn my binoculars around. She becomes smaller and smaller. In the end she will disappear in the waves!"

Compare this to what you do when you are in a mood of depreciation. You are at dinner with business partners in an exquisite restaurant. A small drop of sauce falls on your tie. You clean it with a little water from your glass. Only a slight stain remains, but you blow it out of proportion: "How awful! What must they think. I'm a real slob. These guys will always see me as a man with no table manners."

In a few minutes, you manage to turn a simple mistake into a nightmare. Instead of magnifying what is good about you, you turn your binoculars around to decrease your worth until it disappears like the mother-in-law in the ocean.

### Emotional Appraisal

It is important to appraise your field of life not only on the basis of what is happening here and now, but also in regard to how you feel about it. There is much truth in the fact that if you think things will go the wrong way for you, they often do turn out badly. This appraisal takes a wrong turn because your feelings are the result of your thoughts and not the other way around. Examples of emotional appraisal are: "I feel anxious; therefore, someone must be trying to do something bad to me." "I feel that I cannot do well in tests; therefore, I must be a dumb student." "I feel that this person is trying to control me; therefore, she is dangerous, and I need to run whenever she is around."

If you repeatedly live, think, and act depreciatively, ask yourself: Am I living by feelings or facts? Because you feel badly about things, you take it for granted that they really are bad. Try for a change to question the assumptions that give rise to such feelings. Dig up the hidden appraisals that are the source of your misleading emotions. If you cannot do so by yourself alone, ask a friend, a counselor, or a spiritual director to help you.

Appraisals rooted in averse emotions can make you delay a

task endlessly. The student who tells herself, "I feel so bad about the paper I have to write for my course that it seems almost impossible to make a start of it," will soon be the victim of a self-fulfilling prophecy of procrastination.

## Ought Appraisals

Your "formation conscience" contains the "oughts" that direct the form you give to your life. A healthy conscience is flexible, relaxed, and adaptable to the changing situations you encounter in your field of life. If your formation conscience has grown beyond the functional dimension, you have a better chance of making consonant decisions.

Life comes to a halt in many ways if you do not function well. Functional reason enables you to put your everyday life in order in a practical way. Your functional mind processes directives and decisions that facilitate your ability to manage the practical aspects of life. However, the functional mind should not become so dominant that it suppresses your free spirit.

The oughts that direct you should not be inscribed blindly in your mind like letters engraved in stone. Your spirit will rebel under the pressures of a predominantly functional mind. At some level, if this happens, you feel inhuman and unhappy.

Functionalistic ought directives have a way of spreading out to others. When you fail to live up to what *they* expect of you, you feel resentful of them and testy with yourself. Why should others be free of the oughts that pressure you all the time?

When a teacher is late for class, the self-centered student thinks, "He ought to be on time. He only cares about himself." As a result, the student is in a bad mood during class. This swing to the negative depletes some of the energy that would have helped him to follow the lecture.

Functionalistic ought appraisals are like frozen blocks of ice. Not only are they rigid; they may also be more or less out of tune with reality. They have an obsessive bent. Because their nature is to compel you inflexibly, they are a source of friction and tension. When you fall short of the demands of these compulsive oughts, you end up hating yourself for your failure. Your defeat gives rise to obsessive guilt directives. When others do not live up to the rigid "ought system" that rules you, you feel judgmental, condemnatory, and self-righteous toward them. If you do not gain insight into the functionalistic appraisal dispositions behind these directives, you will feel let down by yourself and others time and again.

## Branding Yourself and Others

Friends in Arizona invited us to their ranch to conduct a retreat. One of the things we saw there was the branding of newborn calves. Using a hot iron, the foreman of the crew burned the family insignia into their skin so that anyone would know to whom the cattle belonged. While branding people, as happened during the horror of the Holocaust, is a despicable practice, its effect may be felt when you, so to speak, burn ideas and images about yourself and other people into your mind and heart.

Branding in this sense means identifying yourself as basically flawed. When you do not get the applause you expect after making a dinner speech, you label yourself as "not a good speaker after all." You make up your mind never to do this kind of thing again. You could have said instead, "The talk did not come off as well as I had hoped. No matter. It is a rehearsal for the next time when I shall do better because of this experience."

When the paper a student wrote for a course received the grade of "B" instead of the "A" she expected, she concluded: "I guess that does it. I'm a 'B' student from now on." What a difference it might have made had she said: "So I got a 'B' for this paper. Next time I'll improve my writing and research and try for an 'A.' It does not mean I'm forever branded a 'B' student."

Branding ourselves with a mark of depreciation is another fallout from one-sided functionalistic appraisal. The free human spirit transcends the determination of being worthwhile only on the basis of what one does. Our life is far more than a matter of technically functioning well. We are human beings, not human doings. Who you are cannot be frozen in the framework of something as unimportant as a momentary failure or a less competitive classroom performance.

Any time we label others as we label ourselves, we risk arousing their anger. An example would be the husband who sees his wife weeping occasionally and brands her "a cry baby." Fixated on this label, he feels irritated by her "weakness." He jumps at every chance to make her feel how vulnerable she is. She in turn labels him a "male pig." They look at each other more and more with these marks branded in their mind. Seeing only what fits their tags, they miss the transcendent beauty of the whole person.

### Blaming Yourself for Others' Misfortunes or Mistakes

This source of twisted appraisal compels you to take responsibility for the bad things that happen around you, even if they are caused by others. When a student complains about a class, an insecure teacher may feel guilty due to the depreciative disposition of self-blaming appraisal. "I must be a poor teacher. It's my fault that he cannot follow my explanations. I am to blame; its my responsibility to make sure that every student understands what I am saying."

When a mother discovers that her child is unable to relate to others, she may berate herself by thinking, "I must have done something bad to cause this to happen. I'm a mother lacking in love. For what other reason would my child withdraw?"

Self-blaming appraisal fills you with false guilt. You become the victim of an unreasonable sense of accountability for anything bad or unpleasant that happens. If you are a woman abused by your husband, you may blame yourself for his gross behavior. "I must not have been kind and helpful enough." When your child becomes drug addicted, your first thought may be, "I must have failed to bring him up the right way." You forget that this boy or girl has a free will. You can never force him or her to do the right thing. Even God does not do that. What children do with their life is their responsibility in the long run. Parents can try to set a good example, but they cannot guarantee the results. They can help their sons and daughters to do better, but they cannot compel them to choose what is best for them.

These ten ways by which appraisal becomes twisted are the sources of many depreciative judgments and the bad feelings that flow from them. Insight into their influence on our life will help us in our attempts to live in the light of the power of appreciative appraisal. This is a work that never ends.

All of us will be caught repeatedly in the snare of compulsive depreciation or wrongly directed appreciation. That is why we insist that right appraisal is the key to understanding our thoughts, moods, and feelings, to finding our way out of the twists that distort transcendent peace and joy.

Appraisal is an act of the will, a discipline of the spirit. It represents a choice, an option: either to direct our thinking and feeling to new depths of candor, courage, and commitment or to become what M. Scott Peck calls "people of the lie." To see life as precious, as highly prized and worthy of praise, is to become instead people who pursue the truth, who affix a high price to the dignity of each person, and who incorporate into their lives of imagining, knowing, feeling, and striving the creative power of profound appreciation.

### HOW TO DETECT SOURCES OF MISDIRECTED APPRAISAL

1. **Listen with loving attention to what any dimension of life is telling you and do not distort realistic directives.**

2. **Take into account the field-directed messages, not the misdirections, that bear on your appraisals, decisions, and actions here and now.**

3. **The moment your obsessions begin to stir, try to temper the narrow judgments behind them that trigger erroneous patterns of response.**

4. **Free yourself from the tyranny of emotions that entrap you in inflexible patterns of depreciative reasoning.**

5. **Do not let yourself be dominated by "oughts," labels, or other marks of depreciation that miss the transcendent beauty of the whole person.**

6. **To disentangle from the twists of distorted directives, make the power of appreciative appraisal your guiding light.**

*Opposition*

*is*

*no*

*cause*

*for*

*defeat.*

## Chapter 9

# Listening to Life Appreciatively

**A**s we have seen, depreciative dispositions give rise to wrong directives that may alienate us not only from the transcendent but also from one another. Yet in our heart of hearts we yearn for wholeness. We long to be in communion with the mystery of all that is. We want to experience peace and purpose, happiness and harmony. Sadly, as the years go by, many people find that their lives and the lives of those dear to them remain undeniably alienated, broken, and wounded. What accounts for this recurrent dissonance?

### The Role of Tradition

Our capacity to listen appreciatively to the appeal of the transcendent is fractured by a plethora of pushes and pulls, trends and threats to which we are exposed daily. The free-floating traditions of consumerism, economism, hedonism, and rampant individualism erode our basic faith and formation traditions. When adhered to indiscriminately, these "isms" are bound to be obstacles to inner peace, communion with others, and union with the Holy.

The kinds of traditions we allow to shape our dispositions and direct our lives will hamper or enhance our journey to appreciative living. We can only give form to everyday happenings in interaction with others who have gone before us. They are the bearers of traditions that live on from age to age. The mark of good traditions is that they foster appreciation. They give rise to wise directives for living. These are the practical and prudent results of attempts by generations of people to disclose and develop faith and formation wisdom within an ordinary field of presence and action.

Recall the way in which your children take over the expressions of faith practiced in your family. Christian children learn from encounters at table how to bow their heads and say grace before meals. Islamic youngsters learn how to bow to Mecca and pray several times a day according to the prophet's way. Keeping the Sabbath and celebrating Passover with ancient rituals become part of a person's initial formation in Judaism.

## Ways of Reformation

Growth in appreciative living does not happen automatically. It depends on listening to what in our various formation traditions is in tune or out of tune with our call of life. Despite our best efforts, our actual life remains a mixture of appreciative and depreciative dispositions. The moment we are in a tense situation both ways of living urge us to repeat a familiar sequence of acts that may be formative or deformative.

What if you are disposed to telling lies? You will have a hard time doing otherwise if the fabrication of stories "not quite true" has become a kind of second nature to you. You tend to create a climate of confusion wherever you are. By contrast, if you are disposed to approach issues with the honesty of an Abraham Lincoln, you will probably be known for your credibility

Because appreciation is a lasting disposition of the heart, it is necessary to reform what in us evokes a depreciative response. Ideally, if we listen honestly, inner and outer instances of dissonance can become for us a call to deeper consonance.

For example, a music student who has to earn tuition money may temporarily become a waitress. While waiting on tables, she develops ways of serving food in an attractive manner, but she does not allow this disposition to affect her life as deeply as does her love for music. In other words, being a waitress does not become a lasting disposition of her heart but a current expression of her self in that particular situation.

Dispositions that are continuous and lasting flow outward

from our core form or heart to our current (here and now) and our apparent (how we appear) forms of life. The more appreciative we are, the more likely it is that we will develop from the heart a lifestyle in tune with the Transcendent and with its mysterious call in our life.

Reformation requires continual listening to our profile of limits as well as to our treasure of possibilities. We neither deny our weak points nor take for granted our gifts. Rather we choose to exercise the power of appreciation and thus to look in every situation for some formation opportunity.

For example, in the Gospel narrative of Christ's passion and death, Peter denied knowing Jesus three times. This heinous act was utterly at odds with his professed love of the Master. He had to endure a painful process of reformation. He wept profusely when he saw that his fear of imprisonment had taken precedence over his love for his friend. Only after the Resurrection did the repentant Peter receive and accept Jesus' commission to feed his lambs and tend his sheep.

## Conditions for Course Alteration

It is never too late to appraise a wrong direction and to alter your course. Aiding your appraisal of what to retain and what to reject in faithfulness to your founding life form or life call are the dispositions of the heart we refer to as the "Cs" of consonance.

The first of these is *congeniality*. This means that we appreciate as the greatest of gifts our ever emerging "genesis" or "origin" in the mystery. We pledge to remain true to our unique-communal call as we know it at the moment.

A life of consonance also entails the disposition of *compatibility*. This means that we strive to appraise and appreciate the inevitable vicissitudes of our situation and its current demands, all of which invite realistic adaptation, flexibility, and patience.

Another fact of life has to be taken into the account. This is that all people, ourselves included, show flaws and frailties. We are vulnerable, wounded and broken in some way. We are often faced with faltering situations and fellow humans as limited as we are.

*Compassion* is thus the third "C" of consonance. This means lovingly caring for our own and others' vulnerability. Compassion compels us to go beyond merely functional forms of expression. Only if our attitude is appreciative, not judgmental, can we open up in compassion to the failings and illusions that mar our own and others' movement to spiritual maturity.

These three "Cs" taken together — *congeniality, compatibility*, and *compassion* — invite us to a fourth appreciative disposition of the heart — that of *competence*. This means that we try to remain effectively present to our everyday world. We discover our own life direction by enlightened participation in the lives of others, by working hard to pursue excellence, by using to the full the gifts and talents God has given us.

In summary, our life is meant to be *congenial* with our founding life form; *compatible* with our current situation; *compassionate* for ourselves and others; and *competent* in our effective execution of consonant decisions and actions.

We cannot go far on this road unless we listen *congenially* to our life call; *compatibly* to our situation; *compassionately* to others; and *competently* to our gifts and talents. The more our ongoing formation of life is a conversation between these four "Cs" of consonance, the more our lives will be gracious, peaceful, and joyful. Our whole being will show openness, happiness, and inner relaxed attentiveness to what matters most in this world.

Living in this appreciative manner requires an additional "C," that of *courage*. The French word for the heart, *le coeur*, reminds us that *courage* is a disposition that ought to be lasting. It takes courage to remain faithful to who we are called to be; to exercise patience in regard to our ever-changing situation; to reach out and touch suffering others while seeing something of our own dignity in them. It takes more courage to exercise to the full our gifts and skills, to function at the peak of our performance, and to place all that we do in service of the Transcendent whose servants we are.

All of these "Cs" presuppose in turn the "C" of candor. Without candid appraisal of where we have been faithful to the former "Cs" and where we have failed to respond fully, we cannot pursue or express the power of appreciation.

Living the "Cs" of consonance enables us to listen to the best of life and to become channels of divine love in this world. At times we succeed in this intention, at times we fail. Because we are limited, we cannot always trust our appraisal of what to do, where to go, what to say. We need to rely, therefore, on the wisdom of time-tested traditions if we are to put our ideals to work in realistic ways.

Henry David Thoreau wrote in *Walden* that it is wonderful to dream our dreams, provided we do what we can to put solid foundations under them. This means that we have to assess courageously and candidly the limits and parameters of each situation in which we find ourselves. We have to listen with clear minds and open hearts, acting, as Teresa of Avila did, with "determined determination."

An important sign that we are learning to listen to life appreciatively is the level of our *interest*. This word, from the Latin *inter-esse*, means "being-between." We have to be between the ideals toward which we aspire and the real work required to accomplish them. We have to see that this work cannot be done without the help of others and that between us more can happen than anyone of us could accomplish alone.

To make our doing an expression of our being, we need to listen to life not in piecemeal fashion but as a whole. Life is a rhythm of work and rest, participation and prayer. By cultivating our "inner gardens," we enhance our outer surroundings as well. Life becomes not a dungeon of drudgery but a space of grace where good things happen in God's own time.


### HOW TO LISTEN TO LIFE APPRECIATIVELY

1. **Be mindful of the influence of traditions that hamper or enhance your growth in appreciative living attuned to the Transcendent.**

2. **Listen to and live within traditions that are consonant with your unique-communal life call.**

3. **Identify honestly and strive to reform that about you which still gives rise to depreciative rather than appreciative responses to self and others, situation and world.**

4. Develop from the depths of your heart a style of life that is in tune with the Transcendent and leads to spiritual maturity.

5. Choose to see in any situation of failure an opportunity to reappraise a wrong direction and to alter your course according to the "Cs" of consonance.

6. Aspire to high ideals and do what you can to accomplish them in congeniality, compatibility, compassion, competence, courage, and candor.

*Limitations*

*and*

*restrictions*

*teach me*

*that to err is*

*human*

*and yet*

*to choose to bear*

*responsibility*

*for*

*my mistakes*

*and*

*humbly accept*

*the challenge*

*of*

*my defeats*

*is*

*to be*

*most free.*

*Chapter 10*

# Rejecting Pride as an Obstacle to Appreciation

**W**eakening, though not permanently vitiating our power of appreciation, is the counterfeit "I" of our fallen human condition. The pride form makes self, not God, the center of life and world. Instead of acknowledging that we are dependent on the divine forming mystery, we act as if we are the captains of our souls, the masters of our fate. The pride form obscures our God-given capacity to give praise to the Most High and to appraise what leads us to happiness in this life.

### Deceptive Ploys of Pride

Denying our dependency on a Higher Power blocks our ability to listen to the appreciative dispositions of the heart. The myth of self-sufficiency prevents us from engaging in candid appraisal. We make idols of our illusions. We choose what is uncongenial with our unique-communal life call. Our life becomes incompatible with the demands of the situation. We lack compassion for suffering others. We are incompetent as servants of the Transcendent and utterly uncourageous. The inclination to blow with the wind of every pulsation around us becomes harder to resist. We ignore the accumulated wisdom of time-tested values and traditions and in the process we lose the point of living.

Instead of acknowledging our dependency on God, the pride form inclines us to believe that we can find peace and joy by means of our own efforts alone. We may fall into the fallacy of perfectionism or the anguish of introspectionism. We forget to place ourselves in the presence of the Transcendent. We make the "little beyonds" of power, pleasure, and possession the be-all and end-all of life.

This tendency to follow dissonant, depreciative dispositions may become pervasive and permanent. We may start to listen mostly to alien directives. Before long we develop a counterfeit form of life. It operates in foolish isolation from our unique-communal call.

The "C" of candor is dimmed by a fondness for lies and false self-talk. We deny what is really true. Like a skilled addict, we lie to others in the hope that they will enable our destructive habit. The "C" of congeniality is replaced by the counterfeit "C" of envious comparison. Compatibility degenerates into backbiting competition. Compassion weakens under a barrage of judgmentalism. Competence becomes an excuse to use others to suit our own ends.

The divine direction of life is perverted by the deceptive ploys of the pride form. Instead of listening to life as a gracious invitation from a loving God, we attend only to our own ego and its willful claims. Me-ism saps life of transcendent meaning. In trying to seclude ourselves from the light of the forming mystery, in sealing off our heart from the gentle whispers of God's will, we succeed only in losing the way. We are like children wandering in a forest overgrown with weeds. The sun is unable to penetrate the dense brush. Soon darkness blocks the light, and we feel afraid, adrift, and alone.

## In Search of Epiphanic Meaning

In our confusion we stretch toward the beckoning clarity of the Transcendent like a morning glory opening to the sun. In our aridity divine grace pours down like dew from the heavens. However dimmed our hearing may be by the raucous clatter of our pride form, in the core of our being we can still respond in humility to the invitation of grace. We can say "yes" to the still small voice reverberating in the innermost recesses of our being and in the events transpiring around us day by day.

At gratuitous moments, when we least expect it, our journey toward appreciative living may again soar upward on wings of love. We sense anew that all the dimensions and spheres of our existence are moving together in a dance of grace. We acknowledge with awe the courage of people who suffer with dignity and do not lose hope. We behold in humble admiration the magnificent expanse of the whole cosmos as an epiphany of the mystery.

The more we transcend the illusion of self-sufficiency, the more we are able to contemplate the divine presence permeating our fragile being and bestowing strength for the journey.

For the Christian, it is the Christ form within that enables us to die to the pride form. It is the Holy Spirit who illumines our hearts, opens our ears, and disposes us to let go of what is dissonant. As children of God, reformed by grace, we strive to grow more like the image of God in whose likeness we are made.

Is not the story of the Samaritan woman at the well our own? Jesus invited her to let go of her superficial notion of a Messiah as only a worker of miracles and a political liberator. He invited her to worship God in spirit and in truth. In the end she was able to recognize in and through this encounter divinely inspired directives that would change her life.

At quiet moments become aware of the creative, transforming action of the Spirit in your heart of hearts. Thank God that you are a precious part of creation, of the cosmos, the earth and its people. Be full of thanks for each moment you are alive. You are not a lonely ship passing in the night. You are anchored in the harbor of love divine. God will draw you through raging waters to the safety of a home port.

## An Attitude of Gratitude

Living appreciatively means being grateful for all that is — from its source in the divine forming mystery to its outflow in every sphere of our life and world, in every disposition and directive we embody, in every act and affirmation we make. To live appreciatively means to cooperate with grace not only when we feel blessed but also when we have to bear life's many burdens.

The here and now is like a treasure chest that holds the wisdom of yesterday, the promise of tomorrow. Past and future can only be understood in dialogue with the present day in which we find ourselves placed in time and space. The Transcendent usually reveals itself through the ordinary like a sudden glance of recognition between two old friends.

To live appreciatively is to rely on the Transcendent despite setbacks and failures. It is to believe that our days on earth unfold like the pages of an infinitely trustworthy text. It is to acknowledge humbly God's eternal *yes* to our well-being and to make this promise the main dynamic principle of our life on earth.

### HOW TO REJECT PRIDE
### AS AN OBSTACLE TO APPRECIATION

1. **Acknowledge your dependency on the divine forming mystery and be willing to engage in candid appraisal of your life call.**

2. **Do not succumb to the delusion that you can find peace and joy by means of your own efforts alone.**

3. **Do not make the "little beyonds" of power, pleasure, and possession the purpose and goal of your life.**

4. **Respond in the core of your being not to the clatter of the pride form but to the still small voice of the Transcendent.**

5. **Go beyond the illusion of self-sufficiency and contemplate the divine presence permeating and strengthening your fragile being.**

6. **Live appreciatively in gratitude for all that is — both when you are blessed and when you bear life's burdens.**

*Only
by continuously
reaching
beyond
our failures
to the possibility
of
fulfillment
can we prevent
the
disintegration
of
our love.*

## Chapter 11

# Accepting Invitations
# to Deepening

The everyday events of life can serve our spiritual growth if we are able to see them not merely as chance happenings but as excellent chances given by God to form and deepen our transcendent outlook.

Certain events in our formation story impact more powerfully on our lives than others. These might be unexpected illness, the loss of a loved one, the failure of a business, war, sudden unemployment, a broken marriage. All such occurrences disrupt the normal flow of life in a startling fashion. The spontaneous unfolding of our current life ceases. Such events make us stand still and wonder: "What is happening to me? Where is my life going? Can I survive this disruption?"

Blows like these bite into our complacency; they beckon us to go beyond thoughtless routines. They are tragic interruptions of life's regularity.

More common are less dramatic events that disrupt our ease of living and throw things into question. Some notable examples might be a misunderstanding between friends or family members; the birth of a child; an engagement to marry; the decision to stay single; the celebration of a promotion; a moving experience of nature during a holiday.

All such sad and happy occasions can lift us out of complacent routines. They, too, make us pause and think about our comings and goings. They offer us an opportunity, as nothing else can, to question the spiritual meaning of the life we are living. How may what is happening reveal more of the rich tapestry of our divine destiny?

## Taking the Risk to Go Deeper

In any crisis we may sense that we are at one of life's many crossroads. It is as if we are being asked to make a change — but how? to what? This invitation is not a mode of coercion but one of appeal. It is as if we are being asked to go beyond or more deeply into some of the ways in which we were disposed to look at life previously. Perhaps we have to give up some dispositions that have served us well for a long time. We have to proceed in an unfamiliar direction — and this is never easy.

No wonder you feel anxious, distraught, hesitant, confronted at once by danger and opportunity. By now these two faces of a crisis ought to be apparent.

You feel in danger because you have to give up ways that seem to have worked for you in the past and you don't yet know what will work for you in the future. Old dispositions die hard. You literally have to depreciate them while passing into the unknown territory that an appreciative stance challenges you to enter.

Opportunity knocks on the door of this experience too. Appreciative abandonment to the divine forming mystery grants you insights and energy you could not otherwise gain. Often the only way to break through the danger inherent in any crisis is, at least to a degree, to break down. Paradoxically, that may be the point at which you begin to mature.

## Making the Right Choice

The many transcendence crises that happen in our lives cannot be resolved overnight. We go through times of darkness before we see the dawning of a new day. For a while we may keep wavering back and forth between danger and opportunity, sinking down and rising up, falling back and going forward in surrendered faith to the new invitations concealed in pleasant and painful happenings.

A common formation crisis occurs in family life when children become teenagers and expect their parents to give them more room to grow. They want the right to make their own mistakes. They do not want to be told what to do. The formation dynamics involved in this event of "cutting the apron strings" are a real test of appreciative living for all concerned.

At first parents feel anxious about what might happen to their children. They are uneasy about what appears to be erratic or ungrateful behavior on their part. Their teenagers no longer listen to orders; they want "to dialogue" about them. Chores are left undone. Peers become more important than parents. Rebellious adolescents may express themselves in rude ways. The claim is that they are not understood.

On the one hand, there is much that is good in this moment of cutting loose. Growing children need more leeway. On the other hand, parents may sense that this painful event of detachment marks the start of a deeper relationship. Something seems to be happening between them and their sons and daughters that will be transforming.

Every letting go in life creates room for relying more faithfully on the eternal love dwelling within. The love God puts into parents' hearts for their children becomes more purified. Remnants of a certain self-centeredness, marked perhaps by possessive care, are overcome as the crisis in question changes one for the better.

Sociohistorically, parents may begin to see what the vocation of parenting entails in their particular social setting and historical tradition. It is an immense challenge to prepare children to live in faithfulness to their own life call and to follow their dream in dialogue with realistic limits and with the great formation traditions of humanity.

Vitally, parents learn that sensual attachment to their children, as when they are infants, has to be complemented by a care that is more mature and spiritual. While this may be less sensually gratifying, it can be uplifting transcendently.

Functionally, parents may realize that they should not feel totally responsible for their adolescents' practical needs. At this age, youngsters must take responsibility for their own way of functioning. They must cease relying on their parents for everything.

Transcendently, parents should strive, mainly by personal example, to instill in teenagers a sense of personal responsibility for their own spiritual life. Church-going gives witness to a living faith, but religion must not be reduced to only an external routine of dos and don'ts. What impresses one is a real experience of God, not "God talk." Parents may not see the fruits of their faith commitment immediately, but their efforts are not in vain. When their children become parents or single responsible adults, the seeds of belief planted in childhood will blossom anew.

As these changes in parental and adolescent relationships take hold, new directions will be given to their sociohistorical, vital, functional, and transcendent dimensions of life. The crises they have endured together are now seen as invitations to growth.

For example, in the functional dimension a parent's refusal to condone every whim may lead to their teenagers having to take more initiative in practical matters. This disposition gives rise to corresponding directives and vice versa. One result might be that Johnny seeks an after-school job to earn spending and tuition money; another might be Mary's realization that she has to clean up her room because mother is not a maid.

Making the right choice at any age has a lot to do with being in touch with our core form, or heart. Deep inside we are all being invited by God to make a basic option between giving in to the false pride form that deforms our life or surrendering to the call of our founding form that does not deceive. This choice for baptized believers is blessed by the Word Incarnate, the Christ form of our life, who makes all things new.

### Flowing with Grace

The option of appreciative abandonment to the mystery signifies your choice to flow with grace. The option for depreciative abandonment suggests, by contrast, that you prefer the ease and complacency of an immature life. You refuse to follow the way of transcendence through everyday events as inspired by the Spirit.

Whatever basic option you make, it will affect everything you say and do. You may make the wrong option and resist grace because you still lack sufficient trust that God will carry you through the dangers and difficulties, the dissonances and disintegrations, each life crisis entails. The mystery in its benevolence will not abandon you.

A depreciative option, lacking in faith, hope, and love, prevents you from abandoning yourself to the mystery. It feels instead as if you have been abandoned by the mystery, as if you are awash in a stormy sea without a lifeline. You are unable to recognize the way by which you can grow and become more whole. Instead you tend to look only for the bad features of a crisis, the danger and difficulty ahead, not the way through it. You see painful happenings as relatively meaningless. In a sense you become a living symbol of depreciative abandonment.

Persons who flow with grace and make a formative option have the opposite experience. They develop a radar-like sensitivity to what is appreciable in any crisis. The dispositions of faith, hope, and love prompt them to abandon themselves to the Beyond in the midst of everydayness.

This appreciative stance enables you to see life as meaningful, no matter what. You wager that there is a good side to every difficult situation. You sense when it is forthcoming. Your whole life gradually becomes a living symbol of what it means to turn an obstacle into a formation opportunity.

### Seeing the Meaning of Suffering

Abandonment to God's loving and transforming will is not a burden but a blessing. The question most frequently asked in this regard is why God seems to allow bad things to happen to good people? How can suffering of this sort be meaningful? The answer is that the mystery of forming love does not want to impose pain and persecution on any creature. God is love. God wants only the good for us. However, the inherent limitations of the laws of matter in the cosmos, the free will of human beings, lead necessarily to afflictive happenings in the lives of the good and bad alike.

In the usual course of life, God does not change or interfere with the known and unknown laws of nature nor take away the free will of bad people who cause the suffering of the innocent. Yet foreseeing in eternal loving knowledge that bad things would happen to good people because of human fallenness and sin, God planned also for the graces that would enable us to use such events — once they occur — as stepping stones to greater spiritual maturity.

God gives us the help we need to enter into and emerge anew from the mourning process, to cope with suffering, and to find new strength. We are granted in the process a wisdom, peace, and joy that the world cannot give. The response of appreciative abandonment heightens our receptivity to divine mercy. It makes transformation, even in the midst of misery, a gift undeserved but graciously granted.

Do you believe that it is God's will to open up for you the door of opportunity in any crisis? Have you sought to deepen your option for appreciative abandonment? Do you trust in the eternally benevolent saving plan of God for humanity? This trust is not only necessary for exercising a formative option in the midst of personal suffering; it is also a condition for coping with the suffering of humanity as a whole.

In a mysterious way — one we can never fathom with our finite minds — God can use an occasion of suffering, once it occurs, to enhance our growth in wisdom and appreciative living. God does not will nor can God ever be held responsible for an event as evil, for example, as the Holocaust of the Jews in Germany. What happened there taught humanity the hideous result of any despotic attempt to repress freedom and destroy dignity.

The lessons of history remind those who promote oppression that human freedom is worth the price of any suffering. This does not mean that war is ever the best or the only way to restore harmony between peoples. We are obliged to do all in our power to alleviate injustice by peaceful means. We must pray for peace on earth while doing what we can to remove the barriers erected by human pride and greed that retard this goal.

Even a lasting loss or defeat can be used by the mystery as an opportunity to help us to discover unknown features of our life call. This attunement to the transcendent quells the tumult in our heart. It hastens our advance to the homeport of appreciative living where peace and joy reign supreme.

## HOW TO ACCEPT INVITATIONS TO DEEPENING

**1. Use formation events and crisis moments to ponder the spiritual meaning and direction of your divine destiny.**

2. Be willing to go through valleys of darkness if it means seeing the dawning of a new day.

3. Resolve to remain appreciative in positive and painful happenings.

4. Resist the deceptions and seductions of the pride form that deform your life.

5. Develop a keen sensitivity to what is appreciable in any crisis by abandoning yourself to the beyond in the midst of everydayness.

6. Try to see times of suffering as stepping stones to transcendent growth in wisdom, peace, and joy.

*The*
*harmony*
*of*
*life*
*goes deeper*
*than*
*its*
*disruptions.*

## Chapter 12

# Expressing Awe and
# Other Appreciative Attitudes

The more appreciative our outlook becomes, the more we stand in awe before the mystery of the Most High. We are overwhelmed by the goodness of God, the grandeur of creation, the divine presence permeating our inmost being and shining forth in our always limited life situation.

A graduate student of ours wrote to tell us that he was "surprised by awe." During a period of intense experiential reflection, this disposition saved him from lapsing into "selfish introspection." He discovered something he had not realized previously:

If there [could be] that much grace in a one-week period of my life, HOW MUCH MORE IN THE EVERYDAY LIFE I AM NOW LIVING! It's taken me ten years to see the grace of a week — and I haven't even plumbed all of [its] depths. . . . I wonder how long it will take us in Eternity to come to appreciate the grace of a short lifetime? . . . I am truly humbled and sit in tear-filled awe over the ineffable mystery of God's grace. [This event] is enabling me to live in appreciative abandonment, worship and reverence in my everyday life. . . . I give thanks in my heart for the gift of appreciative apprehension the two of you have given me (along with who knows how many others?). You continue to guide me into the freedom of transcendence in Christ. Blessed be his Name!

In faith, we seek to disclose the design of holy providence for all people, events, and things. In hope, we confirm the eternal horizon behind all temporal happenings. In love, we celebrate the goodness of God. In awe, we behold divine epiphanic appearances — in minute cells and majestic mountains, in every aspect of creation.

Appreciative appraisal has to include not only a practical intent, aiming at positive results, but also an awe-filled disposition to praise the mystery in the midst of mundane, functional matters.

## Awe and Appreciative Appraisal

Awe disposes us to appraise life appreciatively. To do so we need to slow down, to abide with the divine. The disposition of abiding also helps us to stay rooted in our founding life call. To-abide-with is to wait upon the formative meaning of crises and conflicts. We take our time and try not to rush the process. We abide with what is transpiring. We strive to read the situation as we would a text that is not clear all at once. We have to read it again and again, reflecting upon it.

Besides abiding with awe, we need to be attentive to all facets of a formation event — as attentive as a diamond cutter who may study a gemstone for hours, even days, before deciding how to best release its innate beauty.

Awe-filled, attentive abiding stills erratic impulses and compulsions. It renders of relative value the popular pulsations of a culture that may anesthetize us to the deeper meaning of our calling. These three attitudes help us to create room in our hearts to hear the Holy Spirit speaking in our human spirit.

## Appraising Formation Events Appreciatively

Awe-filled abiding in attention leads to the phase of the appraisal process we designate as *apprehension*, a word with a double meaning. In today's parlance when you feel "apprehensive" it implies that you are afraid of the unknown. Children are often apprehensive of the dark. In classical Latin and early English the word *apprehensio* had another meaning, that of grasping with your mind and heart certain insights that, until this moment, had been hidden. In reference to the appraisal process both meanings are pertinent.

In a formation crisis or conflict, one understandably wonders: "What will happen next?" You begin to discover through deeper probing and transcendent self-presence insights and meanings that evoke some apprehension. The direction of your life itself is at stake. You cannot possibly know the end result of the new current form that is emerging. Understandably you feel a bit fearful about the unknown future. You are not quite certain how things will go.

Many young couples may apprehend in blissful moments of togetherness that they ought to get engaged and married. Though they love each other, they may be jolted by the inner turmoil they feel. On the one hand, they are overjoyed about having met, about having fallen so deeply in love; on the other hand, they are worried about what will happen when the honeymoon is over. Will a lifelong committed relationship fulfill or disappoint their premarital promises and expectations?

The apprehension the couple feels makes them aware not only of the exciting prospect of consonant companionship as they grow older together, but also of the likelihood of dissonance between them for silly or serious reasons. The question may arise: Is this marriage partner really the person who will complement who I most deeply am? It is possible to deny the dissonance one or both partners apprehend, but it will come back to haunt them at a later date.

Such apprehension forecasts the need for a still deeper appraisal. This implies in turn the disclosure of new dispositions and directives. The couple in question may be led to make a realistic option to marry. They may also decide to part as friends or to break up altogether.

The appraisal process often moves back and forth between depreciation and appreciation. In this example, the prospective marriage partners delayed their decision because they wanted to consider all facets of their pending union. What ought they to depreciate? What can they most appreciate?

She may have doubts about his capacity to keep a steady job or to stay away from the old gang and their drinking parties. She weighs these dissonant dimensions of his life against the many good qualities she appreciates in him — his mechanical ability, his warmth and generosity — as well as his success in overcoming some flaws in his character. The same kind of thoughts drift through his mind.

Once the appreciable features of her beloved's personality begin to outweigh the depreciable ones, the breakthrough moment may occur. This does not mean that she denies the lingering presence of some disruption between them. No relationship is or ever will be perfect. Formation for marriage means only that one does not refuse to apprehend passing or permanent dissonance. In fact, the opposite is true. The two of them admit the dissonance that exists between them while agreeing in humor and humility that what they experience together is much more wonderful than either of them could experience apart.

Admitting and accepting signs of dissonance early in a courtship is the best preparation for a lasting marriage. Crisis becomes an opportunity to work together toward the goal of true commitment. The consonance thus attained will be wide enough to embrace the remnants of dissonance always present in any human relationship.

If and when this couple chooses to marry, they will be ready to implement their decision to move toward a lifelong commitment in mutuality and love. In the process they will have to meet the tests reality demands of them. At this point the appraisal process reaches the stage of application or reality testing. This gives rise in turn to still more occasions for appraisal, a process that repeats itself over a lifetime.

### Attunement to Everyday Reality as Mystery

You may ask yourself what new insights may be gained through applying what you have apprehended and affirmed, or admitted and accepted, in awe-filled, attentive abiding? How do these insights disclose new directives to be added to those that have served you well thus far on your formation journey? What strategies for growth in spiritual maturity may have to evolve if you are to cope with this or that specific problem?

Despite your best efforts, there is no guarantee that what you discover and decide to implement will be perfectly consonant with your divine life call. All any of us can do is try the best we can to maintain our trust in the forming mystery as ultimately *for* us.

The specific meaning of a transcendence crisis and our response to it always retains a residue of the unknown. What we are called to be and do with the help of grace is rarely clear to us while a crisis is occurring. Often we have to wait and see what its meaning is in relation to the whole symphony being composed continually by the mystery. The meaning that is emerging is higher and deeper than any one particular instrument can reach. The part played by one or the other crisis and our solution to it sheds light on only a small portion of the whole piece.

Life is like a tapestry. We can see only part of it from any one perspective. God can see the whole creation in a way we, with our limited view, cannot. We simply have to trust that one day we will understand our call — if not here, then in the hereafter. We should never in the meantime use lightly in a literary sense such phrases as "God told me" or "the Holy Spirit said" or "Grace compelled me to do this or that" or "My life call left me no choice but to. . . ."

Mature spirituality implies the realization that we have no chance to master the mystery. Rather it is the mystery that will master us. We do not know absolutely and for certain what God intends for us. As the poet T. S. Eliot says in his *Four Quartets:* "For us, there is only the trying. The rest is not our business." More often than not, we must live in ambiguity and in the simple faith that God loves us and wills our good. We believe we shall receive many blessings if we try honestly to obey the divine will that has guided us from the beginning.

We may come to see the grand design of discipleship in more detail not while it is unfolding but only in looking back at a later date. We must stand in readiness, willing to admit humbly when we have made a mistake and how we may rectify it by means of further appraisal. We may suffer setbacks and challenges but never defeat as long as we live in a mostly appreciative mood. This is the key to consonant living.

## On the Way to Our Goal

You may still ask yourself, "What happens if my best efforts at appraisal do not succeed? What if I take a wrong course — convinced at the time that it is God's will? Then what?"

Faith tells us that even if we make an appraisal that misses the mark the mystery of grace will help us to make the best of it. A potter wants to sculpt a beautiful vase. The resistance of the clay makes it impossible for her to achieve the lovely form she had in mind. Still she does not destroy the clay because of its resistance. She makes something else out of it, a work of art that may be differently formed but that is just as beautiful.

In the same way we see that individuals, even whole populations, may misinterpret in some details of their practical life the directives they identify as the will of God. Often Israel did so. But God did not destroy or forsake the chosen people. Rather God used their mistaken course as an opening to a different, no less fulfilling conclusion in praise of the divine glory.

Try to see the same in relation to your own story. Who you are and what you do are only tiny fragments of God's loving formation of humanity over aeons of time. Each of us is like a passing original wave in the ocean of formation. Our story, though uniquely significant, is but a small drop in a deep and flowing sea.

This ongoing process is made up of what we earlier identified as JNIs, or *Just Noticeable Improvements*. Seldom do we make quantum leaps in the practice of appreciative living. Most often we proceed from current form to current form with strides comparable to baby steps.

The divine forming mystery uses these JNIs to put you in touch with the spheres, dimensions, dynamics, dispositions, and acts of your field of life. For instance, improvements in bodily constitution affect your ability to function more competently. Each improvement enables you to see more clearly what your call is and how you may be able to implement it effectively in your everyday world. Each tiny step encourages you to relate to others in loving, caring ways. Your neighbors are also on the way. They, too, are hesitant yet full of hope. They, too, seek happiness despite breakdowns in harmony.

With each practice of the power of appreciation, no matter how small, you will more nearly approximate the *you* that you truly are. The more you mature in the life of the spirit, the more your actual life form begins to mirror the full integration or consonance God intended for you from all eternity. This spiritual togetherness — this growth in wholeness and, quite possibly, in holiness — puts you in touch with the self you were meant to be, the self God wants you to become.

It makes sense, therefore, to be present in awe and wonder to the splendor of eternal love. Trust that God shepherds the lost and leads the faithful to lush pastures. Put a smile of appreciation on your lips. Hum a song of gratitude in your heart.

However many mistakes you make, however many detours you take, the way to the fullness of appreciation proceeds step by step over a lifetime.

You cannot know, as God does, how each link in the chain is connected to the one that goes before it. Nor can you know the mountains or molehills God will ask you to climb now and in the future. Sometimes you lose the way, but the Spirit waits upon you with loving patience. The mystery sets you once again on the path to consonant living, and perfect love does cast out a multitude of fears.

### HOW TO EXPRESS AWE
### AND OTHER APPRECIATIVE ATTITUDES

1. **Praise the omnipresent mystery in awe-filled reverence in the midst of mundane, functional matters.**

2. **Slow down and abide with what is transpiring in every significant situation while attending patiently to all facets of your life's formation.**

3. **Apprehend the dispositions, directives, and dissonances that will help you to make an appreciative abandonment option.**

4. **Apply the insights you have apprehended and affirmed in awe-filled, attentive abiding.**

5. **Maintain your trust in the forming mystery as ultimately for you despite the ambiguity and uncertainty you sometimes feel.**

6. Try honestly to obey the divine will that has guided you from the beginning, be willing to admit when you have been mistaken in your appraisal, and be ready to reassess what is best.

*The*
*course*
*of a*
*river*
*cannot*
*be*
*changed*
*overnight.*

# Chapter 13

# Choosing Hallmarks of an Appreciative Heart

An unmistakable mark of spiritual maturity, likened to a second conversion, is our capacity to be present to people, events, and things in a predominantly appreciative rather than a depreciative way. This loving, effective mode of presence bears fruit in a fashion often unplanned and unanticipated. Without realizing it, we may exude a warmth and depth others may notice. This ability to be with and for another is a gift not of our making. The mystery uses the dynamic, transforming power of appreciative presence to our daily task to heighten the meaning and the value of those with whom we live and work. The sight of a sunset, the sweet experience of tucking a sleepy child in bed, the first gulp of fresh juice on a warm day — these times of simple goodness are no longer taken for granted.

Our pursuit of the good is sustained by a disposition deeper than functional competence. It has to do with mirroring in our life of service to others the love of God for all people. Our human care, in other words, begins to reflect the care of the Creator. We see ourselves as channels of care through whom the love of God touches and transforms every epiphany of creation. We become more sensitive to the pain and brokenness of humans everywhere. We realize that others — no matter their age or condition — are called like us to be mirrors of the divine forming mystery.

This sense of life as sourced in God, as mirroring love eternal, makes us realize that service to others is not reducible to following a rigid system of anxious dos and don'ts or only memorizing a moral treatise. It is a process of learning to see self and others in the light of a divine design glimpsed now and then but never fully disclosed.

As candlelight in a sanctuary shines through stained-glass windows, illuminating softly the surrounding darkness, so we must come to appreciate the flickering flame of the mystery illuminating each person from within. Appreciation empowers us to push past the barrier of harsh judgmentalism and the egocentric view it breeds. We learn to love others as they are with their temperaments, traditions, and personal histories.

### Personal Hallmarks of a Caring Heart

Previously we discussed four main marks of the appreciative heart: congeniality, compatibility, compassion, and competence. Congeniality in relation to the goal of mirroring the care of the mystery means two things. First of all, we must take care not to hinder the path of growth meant by God for any person. Secondly, we must take into account the life call of others and strive to facilitate their unfolding gently and firmly.

Compatibility in this context means that we have to attend prudently to the demands of the concrete situation in which we live. Our care would have to be expressed in different ways were we, for example, a lay missionary in Nigeria or a director of social service in New York. Because the situations in which people find themselves differ so much, care demands a patient, flexible approach, continually updated by reflection on experience and by reality-testing.

Compassion suggests in the same vein that we remain sensitive to our own vulnerability and that of others. Sensing our limits helps us to avoid a style of care that would hurt or humiliate people who seem to have less than we do. Any form of condescending care violates the disposition of appreciating our own and others' dependency on a power greater than we.

Competence makes us ready and willing to use our wisdom, knowledge, and skills to be effective and responsive to the real needs of others. Admittedly, we are not always willing to deal with the depreciative dispositions and directives still moving our heart. These warp competence, diminish compassion, lessen compatibility, and erode congeniality. Yet in the mirror of appreciation our greed, impatience, lack of empathy, envy, and disrespect cry out for reformation.

It is not easy to walk in the truth of who we are. It takes courage to look candidly at what is lacking in our style of caring. It is human to miss the mark in some way. Yet to grow in appreciation we have to detect where we have failed God, ourselves, and others. Simply seeing what is hindering our call to mirror the mystery is not enough to promote the transformation appreciative living invites. To grow as a caring presence, we need also the courage of conviction. This sign of appreciation prompts us to do everything in our power to reform what deforms our congenial, compatible, compassionate, and competent presence, even if this takes a lifetime of trying.

### Interpersonal Hallmarks of a Caring Heart

Other hallmarks of the heart that enable us to relate to people more appreciatively are concern, confirmation, cooperation, collegiality, concelebration, and commitment.

We mirror divine concern when we express genuine interest in the needs or problems others choose to share with us. Paying attention, remaining patient, and expressing empathy are ways of showing heartfelt concern.

We confirm people when we assure them of their worthiness and encourage them at the same time to affirm themselves. People can only feel good about themselves if they consent to their own life call and dignity. We cannot assume the task of self-affirmation for them; we can only facilitate it by our offer of confirmation. To confirm another is to mirror concretely the original blessing he or she has received from God by virtue of being created in the divine image and likeness.

We mirror the grace of divine cooperation by growing in our ability to respect others whatever their religion, denomination, creed, color, or culture may be. The hallmark of cooperation is to respect the equality in dignity of each human being. It is to cooperate with others without exerting undue pressure. It is to guard against ever pushing against the pace of grace. For example, in an interdenominational context, we would appear uncooperative were we to impose our belief system on others. In a spirit of cooperation, we presume that people are of good will, even if we cannot agree with their faith tenets and assumptions. We give witness freely and wisely to our own faith and formation tradition in collaborative ways that preclude any form of ruthless coercion or self-righteous condemnation.

One more hallmark of an appreciative heart entails the decision to temper our need to assume too quickly a position of authority or superiority over others. Openness does not exclude that at some point in time dialogue has to be brought to appropriate and creative closure. Hence we see collegiality as the disposition of being simultaneously open to another and ready, when the time is right, to move beyond discussion to decision and action.

Mutual appreciation further enables us to temper the competitiveness, one-upmanship, envy, and jealousy that are remnants of our fallenness. Freed from such deformative dispositions by the grace of God, we can celebrate together the gifts and talents given unto us.

We mirror this commitment by our resolve to keep our word in the different tasks and situations in which we find ourselves. The succession of commitments that flow from our life call may be permanent or partial and periodical. Whatever the case may be, they are ways and means to implement our primordial commitment to be faithful to our life call. This is only possible to the degree that we trust that the mystery is always there for us.

Our confidence comes from the infinite faith God has in us. God thinks the world of us. God loves us. Such trust in the unending strength, goodness, and mercy of the mystery illumines and uplifts human weakness. It makes us more receptive to every revelation of divine benevolence.

No matter how bad things may seem in our human view, we believe we are and remain enfolded in God's mercy. However low our human expectations may sink, we are confident that the mystery is at play in ways not readily seen or understood. This hallmark, too, hastens our progress in appreciative living.

## Social Hallmarks of a Caring Heart

We sense that what is happening within us is not for us alone. To be an epiphany of appreciation in an uncaring world, we must be willing to give of ourselves to other people. Their destiny, like ours, is to become a new creation, transformed by grace and alive in God.

The best we may be able to do is plant a few seeds. We may have to be content to teach the way of appreciation simply by virtue of the example of our lives. Faith, hope, and love, as the expression goes, are not taught but caught. Often the help we offer to those entrusted to our care may entail no more than interceding before God for them or showing little acts of kindness and concern. The results of our efforts may not be noticeable, but we can be sure the mystery is at work, forming, reforming, and transforming our limited efforts.

The hidden power of grace at work in an appreciative heart uses prayer and the ministry of presence to heal and console suffering others. Sometimes simply sharing an event or a story becomes a graced opportunity for mutual growth in the spirit. We may not see the results of our efforts to be appreciatively present to others, yet we trust in the power of grace to complete our work.

For instance, adolescents in the average family may seem to be unmoved by any spiritual thought parents try to plant in their hearts and minds. They resist religion or rebel outright. Later in life, when they are fathers and mothers themselves, the seed their parents thought was lost or dead may suddenly germinate and yield its long-awaited harvest.

At any time grace may strike the right chord. At any moment the light radiating from another person may spur someone else on to seek the gift of light within their own heart, where it flickers like a sanctuary light before the sacred image or icon of the life form God meant for them before the world began.

To be an epiphanic presence in the world should never be a self-contained chore. Gracious concern should be shown not only to preferred others but to all. We should extend ourselves in loving appreciation for people whether they are suffering or rejoicing.

There are four social hallmarks of the heart that are linked to the dispositions of congeniality, compatibility, compassion, and competence. These are justice, peace, mercy, and action.

To mirror the love of the mystery for victims of injustice, racism, sexism, or other forms of prejudice calls for the exercise of social justice. Congeniality demands that we give others their due. The ways and means of overcoming discrimination on a national scale ought to be no different from the manner in which we express respect for any member of the human race. Wherever oppression exists, proponents of social justice must find ways to overcome it.

Something similar can be said for social peace between nations and institutions. Compatibility between individuals in a family or in the workplace models in microscopic fashion what is required to resolve the complex issues related to world peace and the prevention of war. Here, too, we are called to be countercultural, for where there is hatred, love must prevail if we are to be living signs of love divine. The vision that all peoples and institutions ought to live in nonviolent dialogue with one another must never be allowed to perish.

Mercy disposes us to extend our compassion for vulnerable individuals, ourselves included, to whole nations, and to people suffering from such calamities as war, famine, excessive criminality, loss of freedom, unjust imprisonment, and other gross instances of suppressed human rights. In each case the mission of compassion becomes a mission of mercy with appropriate works and actions. An appreciative person will often take the lead in such endeavors, not waiting for others to do what is right.

### Conditions for Remaining Appreciative Despite Depletion

The power of appreciation extends not only to the needy but to all persons near and far. Social actions must be rooted in the disposition of appreciative abandonment to the mystery we are called to mirror. In the heat of service, we must not become obsessed by a "savior complex." Thinking you can do it or make it without help from on high is sheer foolishness. This is not the mark of an appreciative heart; it is an expression of the pride form. Imagining that positive results depend on your own efforts alone, you begin to foster the false ideal that you must be available at all times to meet the needs of everyone. The deformative fallacy of omni-availability inclines you to neglect or overlook your limits.

Overexalted ambitions, under the mask of mirroring the mystery, may catapult you into tasks and positions not congenial with your unique-communal call. They distort your ability to become an appreciative presence and lead to the erosion and depletion of social action. The result is that you become exhausted, burned out, and eventually empty of initial idealism. Other symptoms of burn-out may show up when you no longer feel able to do things in a compatible, compassionate, and competent manner. You become irritated with others at home and at work. You are too impatient to listen to their pleas for help. You go through the motions of performing a task but your heart is not in it.

The process of eroding interest often gives rise to false guilt feelings. Hard as you try, good as your intentions may be, you discover that you cannot save the world. A little progress may be made, but life goes on in its old routines.

The more entrapped you are in the savior complex, the more you begin to see yourself as the wellspring of life and energy instead of the divine mystery you are called to mirror. God, after all, is the author of life; you are only a pen in a mighty hand. God is the composer of the symphony; you are only an instrument in the orchestra.

Even the experience of the erosion and depletion of social presence can be turned by the power of appreciation into a formation opportunity. It is good to have experienced first-hand how dissonant your life has become, how lacking you are in zeal and energy.

Depletion, whatever form it takes, can be a turning point in your life. The mystery may enable you to recognize and accept your limits and possibilities once again. You may have to take stock of your life, reappraise your direction, and catch the signs of disintegration before they move toward full-blown depletion.

### Mirroring the Mystery with a Full Heart

Lifted up by the repleting energy of appreciative living, you become more adept at seeing failures, conflicts and crises, imperfections and errors of judgment, as signs of fallenness, as openings to humility. Humility counters the pride that led you to pursue overexalted ambitions in the first place.

Such moments of disappointment throw light on your need for repletion and renew your trust in the power of transforming love. While mistakes and faulty judgments may mar your capacity to mirror the mystery, while these times of depletion may seem meaningless from the viewpoint of human wisdom, they may be exceedingly meaningful in the light of God's overall plan for your life.

To flow with grace, especially when you are in need of repletion, prevents you from fretting about failure. Your presence to the mystery in faith, hope, and love grows stronger as you begin to accept as meaningful each situation of depletion and disappointment. Seeing obstacles serenely as openings to appreciative living is a sure sign of growth in spiritual maturity.

Receptivity of this sort should not be confined to special times of recollected attention, as when you are praying, listening to a good sermon, or seeing a natural wonder like a waterfall or a sunset. The mystery of formation wants to nourish you by the graces hidden in the people you meet in ordinary life, in the things for which you care, in the events you have to face.

In receptivity to the epiphanic meaning of all whom you encounter on life's way, of all that you are called to be and do, you can rise from social activism that is merely functional to social action that is transcendent. You must remember that it is not so much your presence to God as it is God's gracious presence to you that makes such transformation possible.

Despite your limits, grace enables you to mirror God's love and to let this love flow out in care for others, individually and socially. In the end, you must always return to grace, to your being sourced in God alone. Only the grace of loving transformation makes it possible for you to care for others not because of their neediness or attractiveness but because of their eternal calling in the divine.

The power of appreciation makes us experience ourselves not as the origin, the cause, or the maker of social and personal presence and action but as the humble recipient of a gift granted by One who is infinitely greater than we are.

For Christian believers Jesus is the perfect mirror of the life of the Father, who has loved us first. In Christ we are reborn as children of God, whom we call "Abba." Rebirth in Christ makes us share in the Son's mirroring of the eternal love of the Trinity. Baptism in the name of the Father, the Son, and the Holy Spirit lifts us high above our own necessarily limited ability to care for others. As Scripture reminds us, we are only humble servants, only messengers of the mystery.

Christ plants the seed of divine love in the soil of our attempts to care appreciatively. Transformed by grace, our love may mirror God's own unconditional, infinite care for humanity and its consonant unfolding. This love is the sign that Christ himself has become our way, our truth, our life. We reflect the glory of God even as we are being transformed into ever greater degrees of glory. It is Christ in us who begins to love people with the same love with which God loved us. Such charity is the most outstanding hallmark of an appreciative heart.

## HOW TO CHOOSE HALLMARKS
## OF AN APPRECIATIVE HEART

1. **Allow the dynamic, transforming power of appreciative presence to heighten the meaning of your daily task and the value of those to whom you must show social justice, peace, and mercy.**

2. **See yourself as a channel of care through whom the love of God touches and transforms every facet of creation.**

3. **Become sensitive to the pain and brokenness of humans everywhere and mirror in your actions God's own infinite care for humanity and its consonant unfolding.**

4. **Do not hinder the path of growth meant by God for any person entrusted to your care but strive to facilitate their life call gently and firmly within the demands of the concrete situation.**

5. **Use your wisdom, knowledge, and skills to be effective and responsive to the real needs of others, not in condescension but with genuine compassion and concern**

as you confirm their worthiness and encourage them to affirm themselves.

6. Respect the equality in dignity of each human being and cooperate with people without exerting undue pressure, assuming a position of superiority, or exuding a savior complex.

*A*
*negative attitude*
*toward*
*the situation*
*in which*
*I live,*
*if carried*
*to extremes,*
*can result*
*in a life*
*of*
*emptiness,*
*incapable*
*of*
*growth*
*and*
*maturation.*

## Chapter 14

# Exercising Disciplines
# That Evoke Appreciation

To keep the transcendent dimension of our life keenly attuned to consonant directives, we need to exercise our spiritual powers as much as an athlete needs bodily workouts to keep a healthy physique. Understood as such, disciplines of the spirit enhance our ability to be and become good disciples, women and men who radiate love and light into a world darkened by sin.

### Keeping the Right Rhythm

Bernard of Clairvaux, an early medieval master, refers in one of his sermons on the Song of Songs to life as a rhythm of "infusion" and "effusion." In moments of "infusion" we open wide the doors of our interiority. We allow God to infuse grace into our whole being through word and sacrament, prayer and ritual, work and play. Only when we receive the grace of "infusion" are we able to "effuse" to others what we have been given so lavishly by love. First we must be filled like a reservoir; only then can we become channels of grace or "canals" offering care to others.

As Bernard phrases it: First be filled, then control the outpouring. The saint observed even in the thirteenth century that there were more canals in the church than there were grace-filled reservoirs. His advice to his monks is as relevant today as it was when he first delivered it. Only if we are renewed, refreshed, and re-sourced in our divine source, like water in a reservoir, can we fill the space in our minds and hearts with the word of God and be responsive to the stirrings of grace in our everyday life.

## Charting a Disciplined Course

Certain spiritual disciplines, tested over time by generations of seekers on the way to spiritual maturity, are deemed founda-tional. These include:

- Stilling inner and outer distracting " voices" so we can listen to God's "voice" within;

- reading Scripture and other spiritual literature formatively rather than merely informatively;

- practicing meditation on a regular basis and living a medita-tive, reflective lifestyle;

- praying during periods of recollection, in solitude, or to-gether with others in a group setting;

- learning to fill the numerous moments of waiting at red lights, doctors' offices, checkout counters, airports, railway stations, and stores with prayer;

- freely choosing consonant detachments that support our commitments;

- letting go of what preoccupies us — our fears, desires, ambitions, projects, and plans — and all the worry that accompanies them;

- allowing contemplation to permeate action and action to emerge from contemplation.

All of these disciplines demand that we find periods of privacy, times to distance ourselves from the press of busyness so as to step back and gain a more transcendent view.

The disciplines that evoke appreciation challenge us to inte-grate several intertwining planes of personhood. For instance, if you were to concentrate so intently on the rigors of asceticism that you neglected in the process prayer of the heart, you would risk reducing spirituality to a form of imbalanced austerity. You may concentrate on reading Scripture only exegetically or historically. You never take time out for recollected dwelling on the experiential meaning of the text for your life here and now. Your mind and heart, while satiated with information, would hunger for inner transformation.

Examples of imbalance could be compounded. What is clear is that consonance is impossible to attain unless we foster all of the main disciplines that nourish a mature spiritual life.

### Cultivating the Wisdom of Discipleship

To cultivate the wisdom of discipleship, we need to balance work and worship, labor and leisure, action and contemplation. Silence is necessary; so is conversation with spiritual counselors and friends. Formative reading is food for the soul; so are reflection and meditation on life's meaning. Meditation can degenerate into a mental exercise if it is not sustained by prayer of the heart. Contemplation can become an isolated exercise in pietism without purposeful acts of charity. Compare what happens when you take time to listen kindly to a person with a speech problem. You have to slow down. You have to pay attention to every sound and word. You cannot rush the process. Bradley, the rehabilitation counselor in the 1991 movie *Regarding Henry*, helps the brain-damaged main character to regain his powers of speech because he never loses his patience. He trusts that the long silences that precede Henry's first hesitant words are like periods of gestation where seeds of new meaning are taking root. Bradley's patient care enables Henry to recover his real personality.

Before the crime that retarded his mental functions occurred, Henry, a hot-shot lawyer, could have portrayed a person for whom reading was only a means to master information. Now, when his twelve-year-old daughter has to teach him how to read again, it is obvious that this discipline is a formative experience.

When you read formatively, you have to dwell upon and abide with the text at hand. You become more open to receive its wisdom both affectively and cognitively. Essays, poetry, plays, novels, diaries, journals, confessions, and counsels, together with Scripture and the writings of acknowledged spiritual masters, touch your heart as well as stimulate your mind.

By balancing the conditions of recollection and action, prayerful presence and participation, you are better able to integrate head-knowledge with knowledge of the heart. Your thinking and feeling heart aspires to appropriate the inspired meanings of sacred words and symbols. You are better able to follow what the forming mystery is asking of you on your journey.

To know with the heart, we must be ready to see with eyes of faith, to hear with ears of hope, to read the texts of our faith tradition in a formative way. We become detached from worldly information only and begin to live as people of prayer who resist the habit of merely saying prayers in a routine fashion. We see ourselves as pilgrims on the way to spiritual maturity, who need to practice the art of daily deepening. Occasional spiritual delights are pure gifts, but our zeal for God has to be kept alive as well in deserts of aridity.

To cultivate the wisdom of discipleship also means that we must be willing to let go of whatever detains us on the road to appreciative living, including tempting attachments to the consolations of God. We have to seek what God may be saying to us, even in periods of dryness or more severe dark nights.

The prayer life of people in the world differs from the meditative life of monks in monasteries or hermits in hermitages. Married or single people have to find the link between prayer and demands emanating from the marketplace of daily duty. They have to balance family life and friendship with social action and service. Their lifestyle as a whole is not amenable to contemplation as lived by vowed religious in community settings.

It thus makes sense for many to pray their experiences, that is, to converse with God in times of pain and joy, anxiety and trust, tenderness and irritation. It is impossible to evoke and exercise the power of appreciation without this kind of listening.

For example, to build a career is a worthy goal, one that draws upon all your talents. Yet you must be able to illuminate legitimate strivings in the functional sphere with aspirations for the "more than" coming from the Transcendent. In other words, your pursuit of professional excellence must be tempered by prayerful surrender.

The spiritual disciplines of silence, formative reading, meditation, prayer, and contemplation create room in our hearts for the action stirred by the amazing grace of God. The discipline of timely prayer enables us to connect what we do with a deep commitment to be messengers of the mystery. The discipline of timely detachment enables us to let go of useless worry and to seek the recollection that facilitates our receptivity to the lasting values of our faith and formation tradition.

Grace for the journey comes to us through the sacrament of everydayness. We learn from experience, as Henry did in the aforementioned movie, what it takes to become a loving and balanced person in a sometimes brutal world.

### Recognizing and Resisting Obstacles to Appreciative Living

The phrase "frigidity of the heart" suggests a kind of impotence in the areas of affection and appreciation. One appears to be incapable of living a relaxed, affective life of faith and becomes fixated on being effective only. Religion becomes merely a set of rules to follow rigidly rather than an invitation to grow inwardly.

Because we have been educated for the most part in technical, scientific, and rationalistic ways, we may apply the same approach to spiritual practices. We forget that the fruits of prayerful, appreciative living from the heart are not restricted to frugal moments of focal worship. The power of prayer must reverberate in the overall awe-filled reverence that animates our concern for everyone and for the planet entrusted to our care.

The process of inner purification must continue over a lifetime. To practice the presence of God is not a luxury for an elite few but a survival measure in the modern world. Appreciative disciplines of spiritual deepening not only enhance our interior life; they affect every sphere of our world.

The life of prayer could be compared to a fine scent that lingers on in a room after fragrant blossoms have been thrown on a fire. What emerges from our inner sphere is meant to radiate into our relations with the people close to us and with those whom we meet in the community. There has to be a connection between what we pray about and how we live, between times of solitude and distancing from the pressures of immediate demands and times when we use our talents to better the world.

As we become more responsive to divine directives, more appreciative of the spiritual disciplines, we begin to operate with the spontaneity characteristic of enlightened persons. We begin to see from a faith perspective how the parts of our life come together as a whole. We sense anew that everydayness is an epiphanic manifestation of a mystery within us and beyond us. The ordinary suddenly becomes extraordinary: I awaken! I dress! I eat! I work! How wonderful life can be!

Undoubtedly the process of inner purification will bog down if we rely on our own powers alone. Thus to mature in the art of appreciative living, we must understand that the highest point of our journey is but a pale reflection of what grace has already done for us by drawing our quest for consonance into communion with the divine.

The spiritual disciplines point the way to real maturity. They foster as little else can the disposition of appreciative abandonment to the mystery. These disciplines do not deny the good things of life or the lessons to be learned from the human sciences. However, the wisdom of tradition reminds us that spiritual advancement is not an accomplishment of our own doing. It goes beyond what we can attain on the basis of our own formational powers alone.

The exercises evocative of appreciative living enable us to see that grace is always knocking at the door. The mystery never ceases to appeal to our capacity to listen to life from its deepest center. What else can we do but say *yes* always?

## HOW TO EXERCISE DISCIPLINES
## THAT EVOKE APPRECIATION

1. **Discipline yourself to take distance from the press of busyness so as to step back and gain a more transcendent view.**

2. **Take time out for recollected dwelling on the meaning for your life of biblical and classical texts and be open to receive their wisdom both affectively and cognitively.**

3. Worship and work as one who resists the habit of saying prayers in a routine fashion. Become a woman or man of living prayer.

4. Keep your zeal for the Most High as alive in deserts of aridity as on mountaintops of spiritual delights.

5. Make sure that the spiritual disciplines of silence, formative reading, meditation, prayer, and contemplation create room in your heart for the actions stirred by the amazing grace of God.

6. See from a faith perspective how the parts of your life come together as a whole and begin to operate with the spontaneity characteristic of spiritually enlightened disciples, who listen to life from its deepest center.

*If*
*we accept*
*life*
*wholeheartedly*
*as a gift*
*which points*
*beyond itself,*
*our*
*suffering,*
*disappointment,*
*and*
*failure*
*can become as*
*meaningful*
*as*
*our joy.*

## Chapter 15

# Striving Always
# to Live Appreciatively

Grace beckons us out of stale complacency to a life of transcendent transformation. Psychological maturity alone will not make us content. We need to grow at the same time in the spiritual maturity that is our distinct destiny.

One sure sign of our becoming spiritually mature is balance: to serve others while setting aside time to rest; to foster community while respecting our own and others' need for privacy; to be faithful to our life call without becoming frantic about failure; to be detached from excessive elation without falling into inordinate despondency.

### Facilitating Life's Flow Firmly and Gently

Two other dispositions facilitate growth in appreciative living, spiritual maturity, and social effectiveness. These are gentleness and firmness.

Grace calls us to transcendent transformation, yet our response to this gift meets with countless resistances. Some are so subtle they may go unnoticed, others so formidable they seem overwhelming. Any resistance, if not submitted to appreciative appraisal, will hinder the flow of the human spirit as drawn upward by the Holy Spirit. Unappraised depreciative tendencies diminish our chances of coping firmly with the resistances that stand in the way of appreciative living.

You could compare life's ongoing formation with a river winding its way through sturdy rocks. The water ripples and splashes incessantly against boulders that would halt its rush, but it flows on, carving its course through steep slopes and stony banks. Without these resistances, the river would not be able to shape and form the rushing water. It is exactly the interchange between the river and that which would block its flow that grants any body of water its unique contours, its beauty and power. Without resistances the water would rush shapelessly along, soon to be absorbed by surrounding fields. It might even become an ugly swamp without sparkle.

Our life, like a river, must flow in consonance with the dance of formation in time and space. The mystery manifests itself in the resistances everyday life poses as long as these are beheld appreciatively as challenges and invitations to ongoing growth. Life without resistances and the firmness of dealing with them would soon become like a stagnant pool, sluggish and putrid, unable to reflect the sun.

An effortless life without firmness might signal spiritual paralysis. Firmness helps us to find ways of responding creatively and appreciatively to obstacles. We behold these not as sources of distress and despondency but as appeals and challenges to take a firm grip on ourselves and begin to do what is necessary to turn our life around.

Firmness could deteriorate into a willful harshness, characterized by the aim of whipping ourselves and others into shape, were it not complemented by the disposition of gentleness. A gentle lifestyle keeps firmness in check. It prevents us from becoming uncaring or insensitive to the point of rudeness. Gentleness rescues us from impetuous overexertion or a destructive style of asceticism, lacking any semblance of moderation. In short, firmness without gentleness deteriorates into severity; gentleness without firmness betrays itself in an inclination to lose courage and forsake commitments.

A gentle lifestyle cannot be compelled or controlled. Otherwise it may degenerate into a façade of pseudo-gentility. True gentleness expresses itself spontaneously in an encouraging smile, a comforting embrace, a cordial handshake, a considerate ges-

ture, a sensitive choice of tactful words, a serene movement of
the body, a peaceful facial expression. Such ordinary marks of
gentleness, complemented by effective acts of generosity, make
this a lasting sign of an appreciative heart.

### Staying on the Path of Fidelity to Our Call

What is precious to us, and yet what is also frail and easily
wounded, arouses feelings of gentle concern. A tender heart cannot help but be touched by the plight of an immigrant family; a
stranger lost and looking helpless in a bus station; an abandoned
child with no prospect of adoption; a protestor carted away and
beaten because he or she participated in a demonstration for
justice.

Your best potential for practicing the power of appreciation
may be paralyzed by lack of gentleness, also toward yourself. Often you are your own worst enemy. You scoff at the depth of your
own fragility and woundedness. You do not tread gently onto the
path of fidelity. You run excitedly or anxiously, oblivious to wolves
in sheep's clothing who would seduce you to betray your call.

Once the disposition of gentleness begins to pervade your
life, you will be more inclined to see every person as a mirror
of the mystery. You more easily attune your inner ears to the
whisper of the Holy in your heart. You are able at moments of disappointment, shame, and guilt to nurse your wounded feelings
compassionately and kindly. Gentleness is the mild and propi-
tious climate in which the divine presence makes itself known in
the ordinariness of everyday life.

### Finding Joy in the Sorrows of Living

To pursue a life of appreciation portends the dispositions of
patient endurance as well as prolonged joy. Poets like George
Herbert have meditated upon the paradox that at one and the
same time a person can be suffering and yet experience an inex-
plicable lightness of being. In his famous poem "Easter-Wings,"
written in the shape of a butterfly, he writes: "Affliction shall advance the flight in me." An old proverb has it that only through

adversity can we see the stars. How is it possible that in the midst of suffering one can experience joy?

There are myriad portals to this mystery. A mother may find joy in her newborn as a gift of God; a sailor may enjoy the beauty of a carrier cleaving the waves like a carefree dancer under a canopy of stars; a lover may be thrilled by joy when gazing on his beloved as a living symbol of eternal beauty.

We may especially be drawn to appreciative abandonment when life becomes a nightmare of sorrow, loss, and failure. Pain and disappointment, illness and death may be appraised in faith as announcements of the mystery of dying and rising embodied for believers in Jesus Christ. The savior of the world taught by example that a grain of wheat has to be buried in the earth before it can bear a harvest.

A challenging affirmation emerging from the teachings of Christ assures us that God will not leave us orphaned; that God invites us not to be anxious about the morrow; that God's grace is enough to see us through the day.

All of these messages of hope reveal that God cares for us dearly, especially when we are suffering. God does not want innocent people to be victims of the bad choices others make and the cruelty that sometimes results. That such awful things happen every day in many families violates God's intention for our happiness and joy.

Because we are created free, God does not interfere — as would a puppeteer — in human decisions that often lead to painful, debilitating consequences. What God does promise is that we shall be given, if we are open to the energy of divine love, the grace we need to cope with situations beyond our control.

That God will comfort us in our moment of need is heard again and again in the stories of adult children of alcoholics, of women who have been victims of psychological and physical abuse, of participants in various twelve-step programs.

No matter what occurs God wants us to trust in a care beyond all evidence of human cruelty; in a love which is lasting; in a promise that a glory will be ours that is yet to be revealed.

While it may feel as if we are being tested beyond what we can endure, God's grace is there to see us through. Because of this grace we often end up enduring more than we ever thought possible.

This does not mean that we don't have to go through a long time of mourning, of feelings of anger, bitterness, and disappointment. Faith and good will do not immediately take away bitter feelings that are not under our control. Holy Scripture offers ample evidence that believers can express their anger with God. It took them a long time to say, as did Job, that the Lord gives and the Lord takes away: blessed be the name of the Lord (Job 1:21).

This paradox of serenity in the midst of agony seems scandalous in an age beguiled by secularistic approaches that would try to bypass the unavoidability of suffering by focusing mainly on self-gratification.

You may experience rejection as Jesus did, if not in word and deed, then, by the seeming failure of your life. Saints like Francis of Assisi and scholars of the spirit like Søren Kierkegaard were purified in the crucible of suffering, yet they radiated in their words and writings a limpid joy surpassing what human minds, unaided by grace, can ever grasp. You are thus in good company.

### Seeing Dissonance as a Servant of Consonance

Despite your efforts to live appreciatively, there will be times when you do not sound together with your founding life call but succumb to the discordance of the pride form. Despite such lapses, God never leaves you. A faithful Companion walks beside you on the long road to appreciative living.

You must never deny the dissonance you feel. Though you may try to dim the awareness of its symptoms, you cannot evade the dead wood of inner disintegration for too long. Gently and firmly you have to admit the truth of your unhappy state and begin to turn your life around.

Accept the experience of dissonance as a gift of the mystery. Let it signal your desire to change. Let it be a servant source of reformation. This inner work requires courage. You may doubt at times that you are making any progress, but fear not: God appreciates your good intentions and will help you every step of the way.

You must not be discouraged. You must accept the fact that it is nearly impossible to overcome all dissonances during your lifetime. Life on earth is never a finished story; there is always one more chapter to be written. Life is like a spiraling staircase winding its way up and down a steep terrain. At times you make progress, at other times you regress.

The Venerable Francis Libermann, a convert from Judaism and a renowned spiritual guide, once responded candidly to a priest who wrote to him about his progress or lack thereof:

> You do have a difficult character, a troublesome tempera-ment. Don't get it into your head that you absolutely have to get rid of it. Convince yourself rather that God intends you to live with that enemy. . . . What can you do? Your nature is very bad, but you must live in peace and humble submis-sion to God as far as that is concerned . . . don't be unhappy with your lot. Your natural imperfection is compensated for by greater interior graces that you are not aware of, graces that get results in spite of the bad features of your character . . . that is why you are quite wrong in thinking that the feel-ings of remorse you refer to are reproaches that Our Lord is addressing to you. No, my dear fellow, Jesus doesn't speak to your soul so harshly. He loves you too much for that. . . . Don't talk to me about breaking your character . . . you don't break iron: you soften it in the fire. Don't be in such a rush to shake off your fault. Don't long for it too vehemently . . . that would do you more harm than good. . . . Don't take things so much to heart. Forget yourself and quit all this self-analysis. All these troubles will then disappear gradually.

What Libermann is saying here is that certain dissonances in our character formation may never be overcome. What counts be-fore God is our honestly trying to appreciate them as challenges, our efforts to make the best of them. What matters is that we try to grow gently but firmly beyond depreciative dissonance insofar as this is possible. We should never attempt to outrun the pace of grace; otherwise we shall lose track of the real source of our peace.

To yearn too vehemently to brush away every fly that bothers you may be at odds with what life wants to teach you through times of crisis and discord. The process of formation, reforma-tion, and transformation never ceases as long as you are alive. Life on earth can at most only approximate a call to be disclosed over time and revealed fully in eternity. As T. S. Eliot puts it in his

*Four Quartets:* "We shall not cease from exploration and the end of all our exploring will be to arrive where we started and know the place for the first time."

## Striving Always to Live Appreciatively

The grace of appreciative living enables us to see our origin in God, to hear the whispers of the Spirit in our heart, to respond to the invitation to appreciation in our everyday world. That for which we yearn is but a shadow of a long-forgotten memory of humanity, best expressed in the metaphor of a paradise lost.

Deep within us, like a graced refrain, lives the memory of a life that was more finely attuned to the mystery of formation. The longing for this original harmony, for this deep serenity, never leaves us. The memory of it is the source of our striving to live appreciatively.

For the Christian, life as a whole is a prelude to the joy of heart that will be disclosed to us at a time and in a season beyond our imagining. Until then we must trust that the hand of God is guiding our life on earth invisibly.

The mystery of formation dances through cosmos, history, and humanity. The dance is carefree and playful, a celebration of peace, joy, and happiness. The dance fosters freedom of thought and feeling, a graciousness of mind and movement.

Appreciative living bears the marks of such harmony. It enables you to share in the dance of formation. You participate, if only momentarily, in the divine joyfulness pervading cosmos and creation.

In the eye of the believer, the mutual, forming joy of Father, Son, and Holy Spirit is poured out in the universe. The Trinity as creating, redeeming, and sanctifying infuses all the forms we meet in life while rising above them.

The mystery that is love divine brings every atom and molecule of life into being. The sparrow on the wing, field and forest, hill and dale, all that we see visibly is but a shadow of what will be manifested when this earthly dance has come to an end.

Such an appreciative appraisal made in awe-filled faith grants us a graced and gracious openness of mind and heart. We glimpse here and there in the vastness of the cosmos a particular expression of divine delight. With the poet Gerard Manley Hopkins we too want to sing: "Glory be to God for dappled things...." We too see the "grandeur of God" radiating forth into a dark world like "shook foil" catching every beam of light.

## HOW TO STRIVE ALWAYS TO LIVE APPRECIATIVELY

1. **Cope firmly and gently with whatever depreciative dispositions stand in the way of your responding creatively and appreciatively to the resistances of everyday living.**

2. **Behold obstacles not as sources of distress and despondency but as appeals and challenges to take a firm grip on yourself and begin to do what is necessary to turn your life around.**

3. **Be convinced that only through adversity can you see the stars, that grace will uplift your life with joy in the midst of sorrow and loss.**

4. **Let dissonance signal your desire for change; let it be a servant source of formation, reformation, and transformation.**

5. **Never try to outrun the pace of grace lest you lose your peace and place unnecessary restraints on the power of appreciation.**

6. **Trust in the hand of God guiding your life on earth invisibly and enabling you to participate, if only momentarily, in the divine joyfulness pervading cosmos and creation.**

*Appendix*

# Affirmations for Appreciative Living

*Life*

*is*

*a*

*mystery*

*to be*

*lived*

*not*

*a*

*problem*

*to be*

*solved.*

—ADRIAN VAN KAAM

## 1. BECOME APPRECIATIVE

**Give thanks to the Lord, for he is good, for his kindness endures forever....**

*1 Chronicles 16:34*

**Give thanks to God the Father always and for everything in the name of our Lord Jesus Christ.**

*Ephesians 5:20*

To become appreciative, to give thanks, is a distinctively human and Christian activity. It is good for the body, the mind, and the soul.

To live in the attitude of gratitude gives us the assurance and the hope "... **that God makes all things work together for the good of those who have been called according to his decree**" *(Romans 8:28)*.

To become appreciative means, in the words of *David Ben-Gurion*, Israel's first president:

**To live with a purpose greater than yourself, and to see it slowly fulfilled with the passing years.**

Flowing from the gift of gratefulness, like water gushing from a hidden spring, are revelations that console us in sorrow, uplift us in pain.

> **Yes, the Lord shall comfort Zion**
> **and have pity on all her ruins;**
> **Her deserts he shall make like Eden,**
> **her wasteland like the garden of the Lord;**
> **Joy and gladness shall be found in her,**
> **thanksgiving and the sound of song.**
>
> *Isaiah 51:3*

Such promises, found in the Hebrew Scriptures, might have inspired a person full of thanks like *Anne Frank* to write in her *Diary of a Young Girl:*

**... whoever is happy will make others happy too. [One] who has courage and faith will never perish in misery!**

Anne or, for that matter, any of us can be certain of such consolation because, in the words of the *Psalmist:*

> ...[God] satisfie[s] the longing soul
> and fill[s] the hungry...with good things.
>
> *Psalm 107:9*

For this reason, counsels the great humanitarian and doctor *Albert Schweitzer:*

> ...we must all of us take care not to adopt as part of a theory of life all people's bitter sayings about the ingratitude of the world. A great deal of water is flowing underground which never comes up as a spring. In that thought we may find comfort. But we ourselves must try to be the water which does find its way up; we must become a spring at which [all] can quench their thirst for gratitude.

Again Scripture records how the *Psalmist* remains full of thanks, always offering praise to the Most High:

> Let us greet [God] with thanksgiving:
> let us joyfully sing psalms to him.
>
> *Psalm 95:2*

The prophet *Isaiah* shares this glorious vision of Israel's deliverance from the diaspora of its own desperation:

> The desert and the parched land will exult;
> the steppe will rejoice and bloom...
> Streams will burst forth in the desert,
> and rivers in the steppe...
> Those whom the Lord has ransomed will return
> and enter Zion singing,
> crowned with everlasting joy;
> They will meet with joy and gladness,
> sorrow and mourning will flee.
>
> *Isaiah 35:1–10*

To such biblical affirmations, *St. John of the Cross* adds one we can carry with us through all the ups and downs of life, from the highest peaks to the lowest valleys:

> Well and good if all things change, Lord God,
> provided we are rooted in You.

Echoing this sentiment is the discovery made by the artist of light and darkness, *Vincent van Gogh:*

**The best way to know God is to love many things.**

To this happy thought we might add one of our own:

**The best way to become appreciative is to thank God for everything!**

## 2. ESCAPE THE TRAP OF DEPRECIATIVE THINKING

*Viktor Frankl*, logotherapist and man of hope, escaped this terrible trap even while he was imprisoned in a concentration camp. There he found:

**In a word, each man is questioned by life; and he can only *answer to* life by *answering for* his own life; to life he can only respond by being responsible.**

While Frankl may not have known the teaching of the anonymous author of *The Cloud of Unknowing*, the two of them could have been brothers of the spirit. The *author* advises as another way of escape from the shackles of depreciation:

**Step out then resolutely and apply this sovereign remedy. Just as you are, lift up your sick self to God as he is — our God is good and gracious.**

Another master of appreciative presence, *Brother Lawrence of the Resurrection*, beholds the transcendent where others may see only another depreciative trap. He says to us who might doubt the possibility of freedom:

**I wish you could convince yourself that God is often nearer to us, and more effectually present with us, in sickness than in health.**

This saying of Brother Lawrence's sounds like the old *Yiddish proverb:*

**It is better to live in joy than to die in sorrow.**

The *Psalmist* knew well what harm depreciation does to a person, for:

> **Anxiety in a man's heart depresses it,**
> **but a kindly word makes it glad.**
> *Proverbs 12:25*

Echoing the same concern, that we recover the peace which depreciation makes impossible, a *Maltese proverb* has it:

> **Worry, not work, kills us.**

In the end, whether we open the trap door and go free or close it and retreat to our dungeon of gloom is our choice. As always it helps to keep our sense of humor and to recall that:

> **'Twixt optimist and pessimist**
> **The difference is droll;**
> **The optimist sees the doughnut,**
> **The pessimist, the hole.**
> *McLandburgh Wilson*

### 3. TAKE THE LEAP OF FAITH

Taking the leap of faith means believing, in the words of the English poet *Alfred, Lord Tennyson,*

> **that somehow good shall be the final goal of ill.**

According to a contemporary oncologist and advocate of appreciative thinking, *Dr. Bernie Siegel:*

> **This combination of a fighting spirit and a spiritual faith**
> **is the best survival mechanism I know.**

Turning to Holy Scripture, we read in the letter of James:

> **This prayer uttered in faith will reclaim the one who is**
> **ill, and the Lord will restore him to health.**
> *James 5:15*

Under the inspiration of such affirmations, we may find ourselves asking again: What does it mean to believe? What is faith?

> **Faith is a free surrender and a joyous wager on the un-**
> **seen, untried and unknown goodness of God.**
> *Martin Luther*

**Faith seeks understanding.**

**I do not seek to understand that I may believe, but I believe in order to understand.**

*St. Anselm of Canterbury*

Where such faith is, life is to be found. *Mother Teresa of Calcutta* believes that

**God doesn't call us to be successful, but to be faithful.**

She focuses not on the results of her work but on the love that inspires it and flows from it.

An *Indian proverb* confirms Mother Teresa's intuition, for, as it says,

**From small beginnings come great things.**

When the chosen people followed Moses into the desert, they could not have guessed where God's call would lead them. They went with Moses not because they knew their fate but because they had faith.

**The people believed, and when they heard that the Lord was concerned about them and had seen their affliction, they bowed down in worship.**

*Exodus 4:31*

Knowing from his own experience that faith will be tested, *Paul* still challenged the Corinthians to take the leap, assuring them:

**The present burden of our trial is light enough, and earns for us an eternal weight of glory beyond all comparison.**

*2 Corinthians 4:17*

To the Thessalonians *Paul* shared his heartfelt appreciation of the faithful, saying:

**It is no more than right that we thank God unceasingly for you ... because your faith grows apace and your mutual love increases.**

*2 Thessalonians 1:3*

To believers in trouble, to disciples who would doubt, *Peter* offers words of assurance all seekers want to hear. He says simply:

**Cast all your cares on [God] because [God] cares for you.**

*1 Peter 5:7*

At difficult moments when we lack the courage to take the leap of faith, when clouds of disbelief shadow our mind and stifle the longing in our heart, we would do well to accept the wise counsel of *John Wesley*, who writes:

> ...continue in prayer, and in every other way of the Lord. Be not weary or faint in your mind. Press on to the mark. Take no denial. Let him not go, until he bless you. "And the door" of mercy, of holiness, of heaven "shall be opened unto you."

*Father Walter J. Ciszek*, a Jesuit priest who was incarcerated in labor camps for pursuing missionary work in what was then the Soviet Union, shares in the most moving way what it was like for him to take the leap of faith. In the course of struggling with the demons of disbelief and disobedience, he discovered something tremendously important for his spiritual life:

> God's will was not hidden somewhere "out there" in the situations in which I found myself; the situations themselves *were* his will for me.

> What he wanted was for me to accept these situations as from his hands, to let go of the reins and place myself entirely at his disposal.

> He was asking of me an act of total trust, allowing for no interference or restless striving on my part, no reservations, no exceptions, no areas where I could set conditions or seem to hesitate.

> He was asking a complete gift of self, nothing held back. It demanded absolute faith: faith in God's existence, in his providence, in his concern for the minutest detail, in his power to sustain me, and in his love protecting me.

> It meant losing the last hidden doubt, the ultimate fear that God will not be there to bear you up. It was something like that awful eternity between anxiety and belief when a child first leans back and lets go of all support

whatever — only to find that the water truly holds him up and he can float motionless and totally relaxed.

When we are tempted to give into depreciative doubt rather than to once more take the leap of faith, these words of the *Psalmist* might come as readily to our lips as to Father Walter's. In our personally darkest hour we too can pray:

> For you are my hope, O Lord;
> my trust, O God, from my youth.
>
> *Psalm 71:5*

> More than sentinels wait for the dawn,
> Let Israel wait for the Lord,
> For with the Lord is kindness
> and with him is plenteous redemption....
>
> *Psalm 13:7*

## 4. PURSUE PATHS OF TRANSCENDENT TRANSFORMATION

When we start on a journey, we expect to reach our goal. We want people on the other end to welcome us, to call us by name, not to treat us as strangers. *St. Augustine of Hippo*, estranged for so many years from his true calling, refusing to abandon himself appreciatively to the mystery, was a different person after his conversion. He found out what love really meant. He humbly admitted that for all his seeking he had been sought that much more by God.

To us who are still on the way, *Augustine* offers these words of encouragement:

> The Lord knows who are his own, like the farmer who sees the grain among the chaff. Don't be afraid that you will not be recognized, that storms will blow the grain under the chaff. The judge is not some countryman with a pitchfork, but the triune God. He is the God of Abraham, Isaac and Jacob, but he is your God too. You ask him for your reward and the giver is himself the gift. What more can you want?

Another star in the firmament of formation directors, who offered in his *Introduction to the Devout Life* a guide for whomever wished to pursue paths of transcendent transformation, was *St. Francis de Sales*. When we worry about what will happen to us along the way, he reminds us humorously:

**Drones make more noise and work more eagerly than bees, but they make only wax and not honey. So also men who hurry about with tormenting anxiety and eager solicitude never accomplish much, nor do they do it well.**

In her usual motherly manner, the English seer and mystic *Julian of Norwich*, compares God's love to our being fed solid food by a caring mother — food for the body and food for the soul:

**A mother feeds her child with her milk, but our beloved mother Jesus feeds us with himself. In tender courtesy he gives us the Blessed Sacrament, the most treasured food of life.**

If our journey to union with God, to new depths of intimacy with the Divine, is to be effective, we must:

**Miss no single opportunity of making some small sacrifice, here by a smiling look, there by a kindly word; always doing the smallest thing right and doing it all for love.**

*St. Thérèse of Lisieux*

If we think that to love God means to neglect our duty, we need only to listen to sage advice from another master of formation:

**Strength and mildness, that is the divine action; it is also a summary of all apostolic action.**

*Venerable Francis Libermann*

The word "transformation," means, of course, radical change. What is it about us that is changed? What are the signs of such change? A *Danish proverb* suggests:

**Cheerfulness and goodwill make labor light.**

Another sign of transformation is our ability, with the help of grace, to see opportunities for growth where disbelievers may see only obstacles. After years of treating exceptional cancer patients, *Dr. Bernie Siegel* could safely say:

**Though few of us will win Olympic gold medals or slay dragons, disease can be the spark or gift that allows many of us to live out our personal myths and become heroes.**

Dr. Siegel and those entrusted to his care would surely acknowledge the truth of this *Turkish proverb:*

**When an opportunity is in your hand do not allow it to pass.**

One brave young woman who found in enforced solitude a cause for joy was *Anne Frank.* As she recorded in her diary shortly before her capture and transport to certain death:

**...in the evening, when I lie in bed and end my prayers with the words, "I thank you, God, for all that is good and dear and beautiful," I am filled with joy....I don't think then of all the misery, but of the beauty that still remains.**

Does not this vision of the *Psalmist* make the pursuit of transcendent transformation worth every effort we make, every desert we've yet to cross?

> **Although they go forth weeping,**
> **carrying the seed to be sown,**
> **They shall come back rejoicing,**
> **carrying their sheaves.**
> *Psalm 126:6*

## 5. RECOGNIZE ROADBLOCKS TO TRANSCENDENCE

The journey to the land of appreciative living takes a lifetime. Growth in gratitude does not happen overnight because there are many hurdles to cross. The sobering truth of this *Philippine proverb* cannot be denied:

**Nobody reaps happiness without first undergoing hardships.**

Similarly, a *German proverb* reminds us that **"One who has not tasted bitter, knows not what sweet is."** Life teaches us that these tastes commingle and that as a result we cannot walk the way alone. We need to rely on the love and guidance of a Higher Power, on a God who knows, as does a good parent, what will advance and what will retard our growth.

Sad as it may seem, the human condition validates the "street smart" wisdom of this *Turkish proverb:*

**One calamity is better than a thousand counsels.**

The mystery of falling and rising puzzles us, but as *Julian of Norwich* says, we do profit from it:

**A mother may sometimes let her child fall and suffer in various ways, so that it may learn by its mistakes. But she will never allow any real harm to come to the child because of her love. And though earthly mothers may not be able to prevent their children from dying, our heavenly mother Jesus will never let us, his children, see death. For he is all might, all wisdom, and all love. Blessed may he be!**

A major roadblock to transcendence, a real detour, is the combination of depreciation and disbelief. God can even use this hurdle to help us:

**The disbelief of Thomas has done more for our faith than the faith of the other disciples. As he touches Christ and is won over to belief, every doubt is cast aside and our faith is strengthened.**

*St. Gregory the Great*

When we feel inclined to give up, grace reveals more often than not that roadblocks to belief are but roads in disguise.

**...it sometimes happens that cross winds blow us to a safer coast, that meteors draw us aside from whirlpools, and that negligence or error contributes to our escape from mischiefs to which a direct course would have exposed us.**

*Samuel Johnson*

For this reason a *Danish proverb* tells us, **"It is folly to fear what one cannot avoid."** This is another way of saying that there is more to life's setbacks and hardships than meets the eye. As we read in the *Book of Job:*

> **For a tree there is hope,**
> **if it be cut down, that it will sprout again**
> **and that its tender shoots will not cease.**
>
> *Job 14:7*

The same reversal of fortune was confirmed by the experience of *Peter*, who, though he betrayed Christ, became in the end the rock on which the Master built his church. Thus the Apostle teaches:

> **Rejoice, instead, in the measure that you share Christ's sufferings. When his glory is revealed, you will rejoice exultantly.**
>
> *1 Peter 4:13*

## 6. MOVE FROM ALIENATION TO APPRECIATION

Spiritual growth is dynamic, not static. We want to move from whatever prevents us from saying *yes* to life to the freshness of affirmation. We want to believe, in the words of the English novelist *George Eliot*, that **"It is never too late to be what [we] might have been."**

This turn toward appreciative living made all the difference in the life of the former secretary-general of the United Nations *Dag Hammarskjöld*, who recorded in his diary, *Markings*, the event that changed his life:

> **I don't know Who — or what — put the question, I don't know when it was put. I don't even remember answering. But at some moment I did answer Yes to Someone — or Something — and from that hour I was certain that existence is meaningful and that, therefore, my life, in self-surrender, had a goal.**

To move from alienation to appreciation, we must have the courage to admit our mistakes and make another plan. In the words of *Norman Vincent Peale:*

**Don't ever despair. Many successes have been born from seeming failure.**

The following proverbs confirm Peale's point:

**Before you walk you have to creep.**

*A Jamaican Proverb*

**The more a ball is struck, the more it rebounds.**

*An Indian Proverb*

**Adversity brings knowledge, and knowledge brings wisdom.**

*A Welsh Proverb*

Despite the pain our maturation in appreciation at times entails, we can trust in the promise the *Psalmist* proclaims:

> **Give thanks to the Lord,**
> **for he is good,**
> **for his kindness endures forever.**
> *Psalm 106:1*

The *Book of Ecclesiastes* would have us remember that even when life appears to us to be out of control God has our good in mind:

**Consider the work of God. Who can make straight what he has made crooked? On a good day enjoy good things, and on an evil day consider: Both the one and the other God has made, so that man cannot find fault with [God] in anything.**

*Ecclesiastes 7:14*

It is not easy for us to accept the wisdom voiced in the *Philippine proverb*, "**No earthly joy is acquired without tears.**" Still it is only this acceptance in faith that makes it possible for us to move from alienation to appreciation.

**A woman, when she is in travail, has sorrow, because her hour is come; but as soon as she is delivered of the child, she remembers no more the anguish for joy that a man is born into the world. Likewise in death. We wres-**

tle in anguish, yet know that hereafter we shall come forth into a wide, open space, and into eternal joy.

*Martin Luther*

The disposition on which this movement from negation to affirmation most depends is none other than trust. That is why *St. John of the Cross* says: "**Where there is no trust, put trust and you will find trust.**"

However painful the journey is, let us never forget the goal God has in store for us when we consent, in the words of *St. Paul* to the Romans, that "**...all depends on faith, everything is a grace**" (*Romans 4:16*).

**If God causes you to suffer much, it is a sign that [God] has great designs for you, and that [God] certainly intends to make you a saint.**

*St. Ignatius Loyola*

## 7. SEEK DEEPER PEACE

An appreciative heart is a peaceful heart. This is so because, in the words of an *English proverb*,

**Where there is peace, God is.**

To seek this peace was the lifelong quest of spiritual masters whose words inspire seekers as much today as they did in ages past. Listen to the prayer of one of God's beloved troubadours of thanksgiving:

**Lord, make me an instrument of your peace.**
**Where there is hatred, let me sow love;**
**Where there is injury, pardon;**
**Where there is despair, hope;**
**Where there is darkness, light;**
**and where there is sadness, joy.**

**O Divine Master,**
**grant that I may not so much seek**
**to be consoled as to console**
**to be understood as to understand;**
**to be loved as to love;**

for it is in giving that we receive;
it is in pardoning that we are pardoned;
and it is in dying that we are born to eternal life.

*St. Francis of Assisi*

In seeking to become an instrument of peace, we must recognize, as this *Philippine proverb* reminds us, that

**In union there is strength, in discord destruction.**

*Jesus* did not hide this truth from his disciples at the Last Supper. In his *Farewell Discourse* he said:

**I tell you all this that in me you may find peace. You will suffer in the world. But take courage, I have overcome the world.**

*John 16:33*

Often, as we make our way across deserts of discord toward oases of peace, we wonder if we are ultimately alone or if there is a loving hand guiding us. At such times of temptation we must try to see that:

**All God's providences, all God's dealings with us, all [God's] judgments, mercies, warnings, deliverances, tend to peace and repose as their ultimate issue ... after our soul's anxious travail; after the birth of the Spirit; after trial and temptation; after sorrow and pain, after daily dying to the world; after daily risings unto holiness; at length comes the "rest which remaineth unto the people of God."**

*John Henry Cardinal Newman*

To the chosen people, caught in idolatry, discouraged by the seemingly endless crossing to the Promised Land, the Lord offers this reassurance:

**"I, myself," the Lord answered, "will go along, to give you rest."**

*Exodus 33:14*

The disruptions that disturb our seeking deeper peace not only come from without; more often than not the real dissonance we feel comes from within. For this reason, *Paul* in his wisdom wrote to the Colossians:

**Christ's peace must reign in your hearts, since as members of the one body, you have been called to that peace. Dedicate yourselves to thankfulness.**

*Colossians 3:15*

Notice in this affirmation the close connection between peace and thankfulness. This link is confirmed in a letter written to a relative shortly before his death by the American poet *Samuel Taylor Coleridge:*

**... I, thus on the very brink of the grave, solemnly bear witness to you that the Almighty Redeemer, most gracious in his promises to them that truly seek him, is faithful to perform what he hath promised, and has preserved under all my pains and infirmities, the inward peace that passeth all understanding, with the supporting assurance of a reconciled God, who will not withdraw his Spirit from me in the conflict, and in his own time will deliver me from the Evil One!**

For believers the link between a grateful heart and a peaceful mind ought never to be broken. *Jesus'* words, **"Get hold of yourselves! It is I. Do not be afraid!"** (*Matthew 14:27*) are wonderfully consoling in this regard as is the equally strong expression of benediction in the *Psalmist's* prayer:

**May the Lord give strength to his people; may the Lord bless his people with peace!**
*Psalm 29:11*

### 8. DETECT SOURCES OF MISDIRECTED APPRAISAL

**On one occasion Jesus spoke thus: "Father, Lord of heaven and earth, to you I offer praise; for what you have hidden from the learned and the clever you have revealed to the merest children."**

*Matthew 11:25*

Appraisal in common parlance means to put a price on something to determine its value. Appraisal in spiritual parlance means to praise God, to trust appreciatively in Holy Providence, to abandon oneself to childlike confidence to the Father's benevolent will.

The prophet *Ezekiel* confirms the depth of this divine care:

**I will prepare for them peaceful fields for planting; they shall no longer be carried off by famine in the land, or bear the reproaches of the nations.**

*Ezekiel 34:29*

Like children, we are sometimes mistaken in regard to the value we place on things or the decisions we make. Mistakes happen, but God sets us on a new course.

Once we believe that God's mercy is greater than our mistakes, we can begin to appreciate such paradoxical sayings as this one in the Book of Job:

**Happy is the [person] whom God reproves! The Almighty's chastening do not reject.**

*Job 5:17*

An *Arab proverb* confirms the wisdom of not dwelling on the injustices we endured but treasuring the gifts that came our way:

**Write the wrongs that are done to you in sand, but write the good things that happen to you on a piece of marble.**

As we strive to grow in appreciative abandonment to the Mystery, it is important to let go of such emotions as resentment and the desire for retaliation, which diminish us. Always clear the way for gratitude, benediction, joy, and peace. Such dispositions enlarge our spirit. They make us see something praiseworthy in everything.

One source of misdirected appraisal to which classical masters of formation alert us is excessive clinging to our own way. Why stay stuck in the mire of misery when God invites us to the freedom of surrender?

**The fly that clings to honey hinders its flight, and the soul that allows itself attachment to spiritual sweetness hinders its own liberty and contemplation.**

*St. John of the Cross*

To this wise counsel, the saint adds:

**The soul that journeys to God, but does not shake off its cares and quiet its appetites, is like one who drags a cart uphill.**

Wearisome desires and useless worries are bound to throw our powers of appraisal off course. **"Foolish fear doubles danger,"** says an *English proverb.*

We must learn as soon as we detect the rumbles of inner agitation to let them go. As a *Russian proverb* puts it:

**Happiness is not a horse, you cannot harness it.**

The opposite is true:

**Happiness is like coke — something you get as a by-product in the process of making something else.**
*Aldous Huxley*

Once, with the aid of grace, we get our lives back on course — once we adopt steadily an attitude of gratitude — we will find at every turn sources of life-giving strength that direct us to praise the Most High.

**Indeed, for any among the living there is hope; a live dog is better off than a dead lion.**
*Ecclesiastes 9:4*


## 9. LISTEN TO LIFE APPRECIATIVELY

Many of us have heard the expression, "Life itself is the best teacher." To be attentive to its lessons in sorrow as well as joy is to listen to life appreciatively.

**One should not search for an abstract meaning of life. Everyone has [a] specific vocation or mission in life; everyone must carry out a concrete assignment that demands fulfillment.**
*Viktor Frankl*

It takes a wider vision to see the silver lining in every cloud. The ways of divine mercy seem severe to us unless we look at them appreciatively. Then we may be able to see that:

**... [God] saves the unfortunate through their affliction, and instructs them through distress.**

*Job 36:15*

The House of Israel had no choice but to learn to listen to life, no matter what.

**When evil comes upon us, the sword of judgment, or pestilence, or famine, we will stand before this house and before you, for your name is in this house, and we will cry out to you in our affliction, and you will hear and save!**

*2 Chronicles 20:9*

That ours is a saving God *Paul, the Apostle*, had no doubt. His life story is like a long parable about the peaks and valleys of learning to live appreciatively. Thus, he tells the Corinthians:

**I speak to you with utter frankness and boast much about you. I am filled with consolation, and despite my many afflictions my joy knows no bounds.**

*2 Corinthians 7:4*

So convinced was *Paul* of the connection between prayer and appreciation that he could write in another of his epistles:

**Pray perseveringly, be attentive to prayer and pray in a spirit of thanksgiving.**

*Colossians 4:2*

To listen means to obey. This is the main disposition of discipleship. What we are to listen to is the word of God.

In the beginning our response to this word may be rather self-centered. As prayer moves from our lips into our minds and down into our hearts, a transformation occurs. We listen to life as never before. Our listening, like our response, becomes profoundly attentive and thankful.

**... the soul sunk in God, living the life of prayer, is supported, filled, transformed in beauty, by a vitality and a power which are not its own.**

*Evelyn Underhill*

In such a posture of appreciation, we become more patient. In the words of a *German proverb:*

**[We] take the world as it is, not as it ought to be.**

We learn to live in reality, to walk in the truth of who we are, to operate from the center of our humility.

With the author of the *Imitation of Christ*, we pray:

**O Lord . . . I have nothing save you to trust in that can help me in my necessity, for you are my hope, you are my trust, you are my comfort and you are my most faithful helper in every need.**

*Thomas à Kempis*

The appreciative person is not one who bypasses harsh times and difficult events as if these did not happen. We know that life is often unfair. That is a fact, but faith assures us of God's everlasting care.

Faith enables us to see everything in life not as fate but as formation opportunity.

**The good news is . . . [that] the bad news can be turned into good news . . . when [we] change [our] attitude.**

*Robert H. Schuller*

The change that occurs seldom takes place overnight. We continue to wait upon the goodness of the Lord and to be grateful for *Just Noticeable Improvements*.

A *Chinese proverb* says:

**If you are patient in one moment of anger, you will escape a hundred days of sorrow.**

Though we live in a culture bound to clocks, we may come to the realization a great statesman reached:

**It is not the years in your life, but the life in your years that counts.**

*Adlai Stevenson*

In the end the words that may move us more than any others to listen to life appreciatively are those of *Jesus Christ:*

**The thief comes
only to steal and slaughter and destroy,
I came that they might have life
and have it to the full.**

*John 10:10*

## 10. REJECT PRIDE AS AN OBSTACLE TO APPRECIATION

Pride prevents us from praising God. It inclines us also to take for granted our gifts. We forget to express appreciation for blessings received because we care only for rewards.

To build our sense of worth on the sandy soil of self-sufficiency proves in the end to be self-defeating.

> **Pride goes before disaster,**
> **and a haughty spirit before a fall.**
> *Proverbs 16:18*

One who completely depended on the majesty and mystery of God was Mary. Resisting the slightest pull of human pride, she offered her whole self as a vessel of God's word, saying:

> **My being proclaims the greatness of the Lord,**
> **my spirit finds joy in God my savior,**
> **For he has looked upon his servant in her lowliness;**
> **all ages to come shall call me blessed.**
> *Luke 1:46–48*

Pride fosters self-deception. We pretend that we can go it alone, do our own thing, make a niche for ourselves — all without God. In some way we repeat the Fall that broke our friendship with God.

The remedy we seek, the redemption we need, is not ours to give. It comes from One who humbled himself for our sake.

> **Though [Christ] was in the form of God,**
> **he did not deem equality with God**
> **something to be grasped at.**
> **Rather, he emptied himself**
> **and took the form of a slave,**
> **being born in the likeness of men.**
> *Philippians 2:6–7*

When we fail, we may feel lost; then we must trust that we have already been found. The promise at the heart of the Good News is:

**Hold fast to Christ, and you will *never* be lost. God the Father longs for you. God the Son wishes to be your**

**Savior, your Liberator. In this kind and lovely manner has God freed us from these terrible assaults and trials.**
*Martin Luther*

Christ is the bridge over which we cross from unhealthy and captivating pride to wholesome and freeing humility. The way is clear:

**It is better to be humble with the meek
than to share plunder with the proud.**
*Proverbs 16:19*

In the words of *St. Elizabeth Seton,*

**The gate of Heaven is very low; only the humble can enter it.**

If pride hardens our heart and poses an obstacle to living appreciatively, then the condition prompting the birth in us of a grateful heart is humility. This is so because:

**Nothing is in vain or without profit to the humble soul; like the bee it takes its honey even from bitter herbs. It stands always in a state of divine growth, and everything that falls upon it is like the dew of heaven to it.**
*William Law*

Two of the finest "flowers" of humility are love and happiness.

**At the evening of life, you will be examined in love. Learn to love as God desires to be loved and abandon your own way of acting.**
*St. John of the Cross*

To cling stubbornly to despondency when suffering is to risk losing the peace and joy we have been granted because:

**Melancholy is the poison of devotion. When one is in tribulation, it is necessary to be more happy and more joyful because one is nearer to God.**
*St. Clare of Assisi*

## 11. ACCEPT INVITATIONS TO DEEPENING

**And I tell you, ask, and it will be given you; seek, and you will find; knock and it will be opened to you.**
*Luke 11:9–10*

Our Divine Caller continually invites us to the banquet table of thanksgiving. The question is, do we hear these appeals? At times the invitation to appreciation comes in the envelope of suffering. Then what?

**Remember often that it was by suffering and endurance that our Lord saved us; and it is right that we for our part should work out our salvation through sufferings and afflictions, bearing injuries, contradictions, and annoyances with great calm and gentleness.**
*St. Francis de Sales*

The counsel to endure patiently what befalls us must not be wrongly interpreted. It does not mean to sit back and do nothing, to wallow in self-pity, to put the blame for our bad luck on forces over which we have no control. It means only that we are free to take a stand toward suffering: to approach it calmly, realistically, and courageously, or to sink into depreciation and despondency. It helps to remember:

**Indeed, everything is ordered to your benefit, so that the grace bestowed in abundance may bring greater glory to God because they who give thanks are many.**
*2 Corinthians 4:15*

This attitude of acceptance enables us to see the events that happen to us in a new light — not as obstacles but as formation opportunities.

**We should accept, as we would a favor, every moment of our lives and whatever [it] may bring, whether it is good or bad, but the crosses with even greater gratitude than the rest. Crosses release us from this world and by doing so bind us to God.**
*Venerable Charles de Foucauld*

As we become ever more accepting of crosses as invitations to deepening, we come to believe with the *Apostle Timothy:*

**Everything God created is good; nothing is to be rejected when it is received with thanksgiving.**
*1 Timothy 4:4*

We may now begin to see that appreciative abandonment to the Mystery does not mean that we will always comprehend what is happening to us and why. At the most difficult moments:

**We must put all speculations aside and, with childlike willingness, accept all that God presents to us. What God arranges for us to experience at each moment is the best and holiest thing that could happen to us.**
*Jean-Pierre de Caussade*

This appreciative attitude must prevail not only when we have to cope with truly traumatic events but also in our daily dealings with triviality.

**Be patient not only under the great and heavy trials which come upon you, but also under the minor troubles and accidents of life.**
*St. Francis de Sales*

It is consoling to recall when we are at our lowest, humanly speaking, that is the time God bends down to lift us up. In the words of *Jesus:*

**Come to me, all you who are weary and find life burdensome, and I will refresh you. Take my yoke upon your shoulders and learn from me, for I am gentle and humble of heart. Your souls will find rest, for my yoke is easy and my burden light.**
*Matthew 11:28*

At such moments, says *Brother Lawrence of the Resurrection,* "[We] need not cry very loud; God is nearer to us than we think." That is why with the *Psalmist* we pray with confidence:

**For you, O lord, are good and forgiving,**
    **abounding in kindness to all who call upon you.**
*Psalm 100:4*

To accept the invitations of the Most High to a life of personal and spiritual deepening is to:

> **Enter his gates with thanksgiving,**
> **his courts with praise:**
> **Give thanks to [God]; bless his name,**
> **for [God] is good:**
> **the Lord, whose kindness endures forever,**
> **and his faithfulness, to all generations.**
>
> *Psalm 100:4*

## 12. EXPRESS AWE AND OTHER APPRECIATIVE ATTITUDES

To be distinctively human means to be open to the "More Than."
The two wings on which we rise to the Transcendent are wonder
and awe.

Such attitudes are life-giving, never life-denying. The choice
God places before us is itself awesome:

> **I call heaven and earth today to witness against you: I**
> **have set before you life and death, the blessing and the**
> **curse. Choose life, then, that you and your descendants**
> **may live.**
>
> *Deuteronomy 30:19*

Appreciation is the blessing conferred on us by our always
lenient Lord. That is why the prayer of a grateful heart soars
heavenward:

> **Father in Heaven, when the thought of Thee wakes in**
> **our hearts, let it not awaken like a frightened bird that**
> **flies about in dismay, but like a child waking from its**
> **sleep with a heavenly smile.**
>
> *Søren Kierkegaard*

A smile that mirrors the heavens is worth a thousand words.
A *Chinese proverb* holds:

> **One joy scatters a hundred griefs.**

This attitude delights the *Psalmist*, who reminds us when we feel
down:

> **This is the day the Lord has made;**
> **let us be glad and rejoice in it.**
>
> *Psalm 118:24*

> **Therefore my heart is glad and my soul rejoices,**
> **my body, too, abides, in confidence;**
> **Because you will not abandon my soul**
> **to the nether world...**
> **You will show me the path of life,**
> **fullness of joys in your presence...**
>
> *Psalm 16:9–11*

A grateful woman, a joyful man, are refreshing to whomever they meet. When awe and wonder are missing, the air itself feels heavy. Perhaps this explains why Jesus enjoyed the company of children, shepherds, fishermen. They were simple, trustworthy folks, who knew how to say thanks. They knew that:

**We should not accept in silence the benefactions of God, but return thanks for them.**

*St. Basil the Great*

The following words, so often repeated by the *Psalmist*, remind us once again that it is almost impossible to contain such joy:

> **Give thanks to the Lord,**
> **for he is good,**
> **for his kindness endures forever.**
>
> *Psalm 106:1*

To express awe and other appreciative dispositions, it is not enough occasionally, when things are going well, to say thanks to God. The *Apostle Paul* corrects this mistaken notion in no uncertain terms:

**Whatever you do, whether in speech or in action, do it in the name of the Lord Jesus. Give thanks to God the Father through him.**

*Colossians 3:17*

When the prophets realized the extent of the graciousness of God, mere speaking of it would not suffice. One literally had to break into song:

> **Sing out, O heavens, and rejoice, O earth**
> **break forth into song, you mountains.**

> **For the Lord comforts his people**
> **and shows mercy to his afflicted.**
>
> *Isaiah 49:13*

Perhaps this short affirmation of *Paul* best expresses the awe a heart brimming over with gratitude cannot but feel:

> **Thanks be to God for his indescribable gifts.**
>
> *2 Corinthians 9:15*

## 13. CHOOSE HALLMARKS OF AN APPRECIATIVE HEART

**"It's a poor heart that never rejoices,"** says an *English proverb*. In other words, a heart rich in appreciation is a joyful heart. Make this disposition a mark of your character.

> **When you lie down on your bed, remember with thanksgiving the blessings and providence of God. Thereupon, filled with this good thought, you will rejoice in spirit and... brimming with the feeling of good, will wholeheartedly and with all your strength glorify God, giving him from the heart praises that rise on high.**
>
> *St. Anthony the Great*

The appreciative heart is a cluster of consonant dispositions. As the *Apostle Paul* told the Galatians, "... the fruit of the spirit is love, joy, peace, patient endurance, kindness, generosity, faith..." (*Galatians 5:22*).

An appreciative heart, "... trust(s) in the God who provides us richly with all things for our use" (*1 Timothy 6:17*).

In truth, says an *Italian proverb*, "A happy heart is better than a full purse," or, as a *Philippine proverb* puts it, "A loving heart is more precious than gold."

Confronting us more often than not is the choice between depreciation and appreciation. It is a choice we have to make every day because no day is without its own concerns. The option may require some reflection, but the answer is clear:

> **But once I had brains and a heart also, so having tried them both, I should much rather have a heart.**
>
> *The Tinman from the Wizard of Oz*

According to the *Venerable Francis Libermann*, the two most important hallmarks of an appreciative heart are gentleness and humility. **"These two virtues,"** he says, **"demand . . . docility and submission to God. All rigidity of will, all trusting in oneself and one's own ideas, must disappear . . . if one is to possess these two magnificent virtues."**

The more we opt to become appreciative, the less in danger we are of accepting as our only choice the dry fruits of depreciation. We have no interest in detouring our life on the dead-end streets of distrust, joylessness, anger, and fear. We believe with heartfelt confidence that:

> **Where there is trust there also one can count on love, and the greatness of the love can be measured by the greatness of the trust.**
>
> *Venerable Francis Libermann*

The ripe fruits of a spiritually mature, mellow, and thankful heart are incredibly attractive. **"A soul enkindled with love,"** says *St. John of the Cross*, **"is a gentle, meek, humble, and patient soul."** Others want to be around such a person. The reason is obvious:

> **Because you are God's chosen ones, holy and beloved, clothe yourselves with heartfelt mercy, with kindness, humility, meekness, and patience.**
>
> *Colossians 3:12*

Such a heart is courageous. Appreciation is the mother of the heart's conviction and its irresistible commitment. **"Wholeheartedness will pierce a rock,"** says a *Japanese proverb*, a thought not to be outdone by this reminder from Tibet:

> **If the heart be stout, a mouse can lift an elephant.**
>
> *A Tibetan proverb*

## 14. EXERCISE DISCIPLINES THAT EVOKE APPRECIATIVE LIVING

It is one thing to choose to be appreciative; it is another to maintain this commitment. It takes discipline, but the effort is well worth it, considering the results.

**We can exercise considerable control over our thoughts and attitudes, and can choose how we use adversity and the so-called useless events in our lives.**

*Dr. Bernie Siegel*

In the light of a disciplined decision to stay appreciative, what appears at first glance meaningless may prove to be most meaningful for a balanced life.

**I've found that there is always some beauty left in nature, sunshine, freedom, in yourself; these can all help you. Look at these things, then you find yourself again, and God, and then you regain your balance.**

*Anne Frank*

The way we lose balance is to weight our lives in the direction of seeking answers to every question, complaining bitterly when they are not found, and blaming others for our misfortune. Perhaps we ought to remember, when we are so far off base, the *Chinese proverb:*

**A single kind word keeps one warm for three winters.**

The same wisdom convinced the prophet amid his own hardships:

**Blessed is the man who trusts in the Lord,**
**whose hope is in the Lord.**

*Jeremiah 17:7*

No one should underestimate the challenge to stay appreciative. To exercise this discipline takes courage. We do not make such a choice once and for all; it must be renewed daily.

**If [we] wish to make any progress in the service of God we must begin every day of our life with new ardor.**

*St. Charles Borromeo*

**Resolved, to endeavor to do my utmost to deny whatever is not most agreeable to a good, and universally sweet and benevolent, quiet, peaceable, contented, easy, compassionate, generous, humble, meek, modest, submissive, obliging, diligent and industrious, charitable, even, patient, moderate, forgiving, sincere temper;**

**and to do at all times what such a temper would lead me to.**

*Jonathan Edwards*

Resolutions as remarkable as these can only be fulfilled when we realize that our own efforts are insufficient to guarantee the happiness that comes with appreciative living. We need to rely on the grace of God for this gift.

**He said to me, "My grace is enough for you, for in weakness power reaches perfection." And so I willingly boast of my weaknesses instead, that the power of Christ may rest upon me.**

*2 Corinthians 12:9*

Once we resolve to stay appreciative, we will find that this disposition draws us out of ourselves toward others.

**The only ones among you who will be really happy are those who will have sought and found how to serve.**

*Albert Schweitzer*

As we learn to **"serve the Lord with gladness"** and to **"come before him with joyful song"** (*Psalm 100:2*), we will notice a real improvement in our personal life and our life with others.

**In general you must cultivate a liking for everyone, whatever their opinions on religious principles or their opinions of yourself. You must, moreover, leave them full freedom to think and act as they wish.**

*Venerable Francis Libermann*

This attitude of "letting be" teaches us what a *Hindu proverb* suggests:

**True happiness consists in making happy.**

We may also find that our sense of humor has been sweetened by the exercise of this special disposition. We may see that sadness can be dispelled in a commonsense fashion:

**Sorrow can be alleviated by good sleep, a bath, and a glass of wine.**

*St. Thomas Aquinas*

## 15. STRIVE ALWAYS TO LIVE APPRECIATIVELY

**Let the brothers ever avoid appearing gloomy, sad, and clouded, like the hypocrites; but let one ever be found joyous in the Lord, gay, amiable, and gracious....**

*St. Francis of Assisi*

The decision to live life appreciatively, the discipline to renew this commitment daily, now begins to shape and form our lives in a new direction. We sense that we have begun to **"render constant thanks"** (*1 Thessalonians 5:18*). For the believer it is clear, as *St. Paul* wrote in this passage, that **"...such is God's will for you in Christ Jesus."**

The Apostle returned to the same theme in his second letter to the Thessalonians, saying:

**We are bound to thank God for you always, beloved... in the Lord, because you are the first fruits of those whom God has chosen for salvation, in holiness of spirit and fidelity to truth.**

*2 Thessalonians 2:13*

Once we strive always and everywhere to stay appreciative, it is amazing to behold the good things that start to happen to us. How else can we explain this wonder?

**Going everywhere, my God, with you, everywhere things will happen as I desire for you.**

*St. John of the Cross*

The explanation for such goodness has to do with the person-to-person relation that exists between us and God. We see now that all is gift. We know that what we must do always is to offer thanks to the Divine Giver, for

**Every worthwhile gift, every genuine benefit comes from above, descending from the Father of the heavenly luminaries, who cannot change and who is never shadowed over.**

*James 1:17*

The avenue to finding and keeping the attitude of gratitude is prayer.

**There is a reciprocal and inseparable relationship be-
tween the shaping of one's life and unceasing prayer-
fulness. Just as the whole archway of the virtues points
to its keystone, prayer, so, without this keystone, the
archway cannot retain its strength and stability**

*John Cassian*

Once we move from merely saying prayers to becoming living
prayer, we find ourselves overtaken, as it were, by a God-given
certitude:

**... dead, yet here we are, alive; punished, but not put to
death; sorrowful, though we are always rejoicing; poor,
yet we enrich many. We seem to have nothing, yet everything is ours!**

*2 Corinthians 6:9–10*

Another tribute to the human spirit is found in the diary of a
young girl whose life soon would be snatched away:

**I looked out of the open window too, over a large area
of Amsterdam, over all the roofs and on the horizon,
which was such a pale blue that it was hard to see the
dividing line. "As long as this exists," I thought, "and
I may live to see it, this sunshine, the cloudless skies,
while this lasts, I cannot be unhappy." ... As then there
will always be comfort for every sorrow, whatever the
circumstances may be. And I firmly believe that nature
brings solace in all troubles.**

*Anne Frank*

Two spiritual guides, unknown to Anne, yet at one with her
faith, refuse, as she did, to accept anything less than a wholly
appreciative view:

**Let nothing disturb you;
nothing frighten you.
All things are passing.
God never changes.
Patience obtains all things.
Nothing is wanting to [one] who possesses God.
God alone suffices.**

*St. Teresa of Avila*

In confirmation of the saint's conviction, blessed *Julian of Norwich* says with simple words that wipe away the last remnants of doubt: **"All shall be well, and all shall be well, and all manner of things shall be well."**

The words of the *Psalmist* draw us once and for all past the deadening effects of depreciation into the land of everlasting appreciation:

> **You spread the table before me**
> **in the sight of my foes;**
> **You anoint my head with oil;**
> **my cup overflows.**
> **Only goodness and kindness follow me**
> **all the days of my life:**
> **And I shall dwell in the house of the Lord**
> **for years to come.**
>
> *Psalm 23:5–6*

# Bibliography

Aelred of Rievaulx. *On Spiritual Friendship*. Trans. M. E. Laker. Washington, D.C.: Cistercian/Consortium Press, 1974.

Allport, Gordon W. *Becoming*. New Haven, Conn.: Yale University Press, 1968.

Arnold, M. B. *Emotion and Personality*. New York: Columbia University Press, 1960.

Athanasius. *The Life of Anthony and the Letter to Marcellinus*. Trans. Robert C. Gregg. Classics of Western Spirituality Series. New York: Paulist Press, 1980.

Augustine, St. *The Confessions of St. Augustine*. Trans. John K. Ryan. Garden City, N.Y.: Doubleday and Co., 1960.

Becker, Ernest. *The Denial of Death*. New York: Free Press, 1973.

———. *The Structure of Evil*. New York: Free Press, 1968.

Benson, Herbert. *The Relaxation Response*. New York: William Morrow and Co., 1975.

Bernard of Clairvaux, St. *The Steps of Humility and Pride; On Loving God* in *Treatises II*. Washington, D.C.: Cistercian/Consortium Press, 1974.

Bianchi, Eugene C. *Aging as a Spiritual Journey*. New York: Crossroad, 1984.

Bloom, Anthony. *Living Prayer*. Springfield, Ill.: Templegate, 1966.

Bloom, Anthony, and George Lefebvre. *Courage to Pray*. New York: Paulist Press, 1973.

Bonhoeffer, Dietrich. *Letters and Papers from Prison*. New York: Macmillan, 1971.

Boros, Ladislaus, S.J. *Living in Hope*. Garden City, N.Y.: Image Books, 1973.

———. *Pain and Providence*. New York: Crossroad/Seabury Press, 1972.

*Brokenness*. Cincinnati: St. Anthony Messenger Press, 1980.

Brown, Raphael. *The Little Flowers of St. Francis*. Garden City, N.Y.: Image Books, 1958.

Buber, Martin. *Between Man and Man*. Trans. R. G. Smith. New York: Macmillan, 1965.

——. *I and Thou*. Trans. W. Kaufmann. New York: Charles Scribner's Sons, 1970.

Burns, David D., M.D. *Feeling Good*. New York: New American Library, 1980.

Carretto, Carlo. *In Search of the Beyond*. Maryknoll, N.Y.: Orbis Books, 1976.

——. *Letters from the Desert*. Maryknoll, N.Y.: Orbis Books, 1972.

Cassian, John. *Conferences*. Trans. Colm Luibheid. Classics of Western Spirituality Series. New York: Paulist Press, 1985.

Catherine of Siena, St. *The Dialogue*. Trans. Suzanne Noffke, O.P. Classics of Western Spirituality Series. New York: Paulist Press, 1980.

Castle, Tony. *The New Book of Christian Quotations*. New York: Crossroad, 1983.

Chautard, Dom Jean-Baptiste. *The Soul of the Apostolate*. Trans. A Monk of Our Lady of Gethsemani, Kentucky. The Abbey of Gethsemani, 1946.

Chervin, Ronda De Sola. *Quotable Saints*. Ann Arbor, Mich.: Servant Books, 1992.

Ciszek, Walter, S.J. *He Leadeth Me*. Garden City, N.Y.: Doubleday and Co., 1973.

*The Cloud of Unknowing and the Book of Privy Counseling*. Ed. W. Johnston. Garden City, N.Y.: Doubleday and Co., 1973.

Collins, W. J. *Out of the Depths: The Story of a Priest-Patient in a Mental Hospital*. Garden City, N.Y.: Doubleday and Co., 1971.

Cooper, Patricia, and Norma Bradley Allen. *The Quilters: Women and Domestic Art, An Oral History*. New York: Doubleday and Co., 1989.

Csikszentmihalyi, Mihaly. *Flow*. New York: Harper & Row, 1990.

Day, Dorothy. *The Long Loneliness*. Garden City, N.Y.: Image Books, 1959.

de Caussade, Jean Pierre. *Abandonment to Divine Providence*. Trans. John Beevers. Garden City, N.Y.: Doubleday and Co., 1975.

de Sainte-Exupery, Antoine. *Wind, Sand and Stars*. London: Pan Books, 1939.

Dewey, Bradley. *The New Obedience: Kierkegaard on Imitating Christ*. Washington, D.C.: Corpus, 1968.

Dessain, C.S. *Newman's Spiritual Themes*. Dublin: Veritas, 1977.

Dillard, Annie. *Pilgrim at Tinker Creek*. New York: Harper & Row, 1975.

Doherty, Eddie. *Desert Windows*. Denville, N.J.: Dimension Books, 1977.

Durckheim, K. G. *Daily Life As Spiritual Exercise*. Trans. R. Lewinneck and P. L. Travers. New York: Harper & Row, 1972.

Edelwich, Jerry, with Arthur Brodsky. *Burn-Out*. New York: Human Sciences Press, 1980.

Edwards, Tilden. *Living Simply through the Day*. New York: Paulist Press, 1977.

Egan, Harvey, S.J. *An Anthology of Christian Mysticism*. Collegeville, Minn.: Liturgical Press, 1991.

Eliot, T. S. *Four Quartets*. New York: Harcourt, Brace and World, 1971.

Ellul, Jacques. *Hope in Times of Abandonment*. New York: Seabury Press, 1980.

Ferguson, John. *The Place of Suffering*. Cambridge: James Clarke & Co., 1972.

Fittipaldi, Silvio. *How to Pray Always without Always Praying*. Notre Dame, Ind.: Fides/Claretian, 1978.

Foster, Richard J. *Celebration of Discipline*. San Francisco: Harper & Row, 1978

Francis and Clare. *The Complete Works*. Trans. Regis J. Armstrong, O.F.M. Cap., and Ignatius C. Brady, O.F.M. Classics of Western Spirituality Series. New York: Paulist Press, 1982.

Francis, de Sales, St. *Introduction to the Devout Life*. Trans. John K. Ryan. New York: Image Books, 1966.

Frank, Anne. *The Diary of a Young Girl*. Trans. B. M. Mooyaart-Doubleday. New York: Modern Library, 1952.

Frankl, Viktor. *Man's Search for Meaning: An Introduction to Logotherapy*. Trans. L. Lasch. New York: Washington Square Press, 1963.

Fremantle, Anne, ed. *The Protestant Mystics*. New York: Mentor, 1965.

Gilbert, Alphonse, C.S.Sp. *You Have Laid Your Hand on Me*. Rome: Tipografia S. Pio Xo, 1983.

Goricheva, Tatiana. *Talking about God Is Dangerous*. New York: Crossroad, 1988.

Greenwald, Jerry A., Ph.D. *Breaking Out of Loneliness*. New York: Rawson Wade, 1980.

Gregory the Great, St. *On Pastoral Care*. Ancient Christian Writers Series. Trans. Henry Davis, S.J. New York: Newman Press, 1978.

Griffin, John Howard. *The Hermitage Journals*. Kansas City: Andrews & McNeill, 1981.

Guardini, Romano. *Sacred Signs*. Trans. G. Branham. St. Louis: Pio Decimo Press, 1956.

Hammarskjöld, Dag. *Markings*. Trans. L. Sjoberg and W. H. Auden. New York: Knopf, 1969.

Haughton, Rosemary. *On Trying to Be Human*. London and Dublin: Geoffrey Chapman, 1966.

Helldorfer, Martin C. *The Work Trap*. Whitinsville, Mass.: Affirmation Books, 1983.

Herbert, George. *The Country Parson, The Temple*. Trans. John N. Wall, Jr. Classics of Western Spirituality Series. New York: Paulist Press, 1981.

Heschel, Abraham J. *I Asked for Wonder*. Ed. Samuel H. Dresner. New York: Crossroad, 1984.

———. *Who Is Man?* Stanford, Calif.: Stanford University Press, 1965.

Hillyer, Philip. *Charles de Foucauld*. Collegeville, Minn.: Liturgical Press, 1990.

Hopkins, Gerard Manley. *Selected Poetry*. Ed. W. H. Gardner. London: Penguin Books, 1963.

Huebsch, Bill. *A Spirituality of Wholeness*. Mystic, Conn.: Twenty-Third, 1988.

Hurnard, Hannah. *Hinds' Feet on High Places*. Wheaton, Ill.: Tyndale House, 1976.

Huxley, Aldous. *The Devils of Loudun*. New York: Harper & Row, 1971.

Ignatius Loyola, St. *The Spiritual Exercises of Saint Ignatius Loyola*. Trans. Lewis Delmage. Hawthorne, N.J.: Joseph F. Wagner, 1968.

John of the Cross, St. *The Collected Works*. Trans. Kieran Kavanaugh, O.C.D., and Otilio Rodriguez, O.C.D., Washington, D.C.: Institute of Carmelite Studies, 1973.

Johnston, William. *Silent Music: The Science of Meditation*. New York: Harper & Row, 1976.

Jones, Christopher. *Scott: A Meditation on Suffering and Helplessness*. Springfield, Ill.: Templegate, 1978.

Julian of Norwich. *Showings*. Trans. Edmund Colledge and James Walsh. New York: Paulist Press, 1978.

Keen, Sam. *Apology for Wonder*. New York: Harper & Row, 1969.

Kelly, Thomas R. *A Testament of Devotion*. New York: Harper & Row, 1941.

Kempis, Thomas à. *The Imitation of Christ*. Ed. H. C. Gardiner. Garden City, N.Y.: Doubleday and Co., Image Books, 1965.

Kierkegaard, Søren. *Purity of Heart Is to Will One Thing*. Trans. D. Steere. New York: Harper & Row, 1956.

Lapierre, Dominique. *The City of Joy*. Trans. Kathryn Spink. New York: Warner Books, 1985.

*Laughter, The Best Medicine*. Ed. Reader's Digest. New York: Berkley Books, 1985.

Law, William. *A Serious Call to a Devout and Holy Life, The Spirit of Love*. Classics of Western Spirituality Series. New York: Paulist Press, 1978.

Lawrence of the Resurrection, Brother. *The Practice of the Presence of God*. Trans. Donald Attwater. Springfield, Ill.: Templegate, 1976.

Leech, Kenneth. *True Prayer*. San Francisco: Harper & Row, 1980.

Leslie, Reo N. *Peace in Troubled Waters*. Lima, Ohio: Fairway Press, 1987.

LeFevre, Perry D., ed. *The Prayers of Kierkegaard*. Chicago: University of Chicago Press, 1963.

Le Joly, Edward. *Servant of Love: Mother Teresa and Her Missionaries of Charity*. San Francisco: Harper & Row, 1977.

Lewis, C. S. *Surprised by Joy*. New York: Harcourt, Brace and World, 1955.

——. *The Problem of Pain*. New York: Macmillan, 1968.

Libermann, Francis. *Spiritual Letters to Clergy and Religious*. 3 vols. Trans. Walter Van de Putte. Pittsburgh: Duquesne University Press, 1963–66.

Lindbergh, Anne Morrow. *Gift from the Sea*. New York: Vintage Books, 1965.

Llewelyn, Robert, ed. *The Joy of the Saints*. Springfield, Ill.: Templegate, 1989.

Luther, Martin. *The Theologia Germanica of Martin Luther*. Trans. Bengt Hoffman. Classics of Western Spirituality Series. New York: Paulist Press, 1980.

Lynch, James. *The Broken Heart: The Medical Consequences of Loneliness*. New York: Basic Books, 1977.

Lynch, William F. *Images of Hope*. Notre Dame: University of Notre Dame Press, 1965.

McGinnis, Alan Loy. *The Power of Optimism*. San Francisco: Harper & Row, 1990.

McNeill, Donald P., et al. *Compassion*. Garden City, N.Y.: Doubleday and Co., 1982.

Maloney, George A. *Inward Stillness*. Denville, N.J.: Dimension Books, 1976.

Martorano, Joseph T., and John P. Kildahlm. *Beyond Negative Thinking*. New York: Plenum Press, 1989.

May, Gerald G. *Care of Mind/Care of Spirit*. San Francisco: Harper & Row, 1982.

Merton, Thomas. *The Sign of Jonas*. Garden City, N.Y.: Doubleday and Co., 1956.

Metz, J. B. *Poverty of Spirit*. Trans. J. Drury. Paramus, N.J.: Newman Press, 1970.

Mieder, Wolfgang. *The Prentice-Hall Encyclopedia of World Proverbs*. Englewood Cliffs, N.J.: Prentice-Hall, 1986.

Moody, Raymond, Jr. *Life after Life*. New York: Bantam Books, 1976.

Moustakas, Clarke E. *Creativity and Conformity*. Princeton, N.J.: Van Nostrand, 1967.

Muggeridge, Malcolm. *Something Beautiful for God*. London: Collins Clear-Type Press, 1974.

Muto, Susan A. *Blessings That Make Us Be*. New York: Crossroad, 1982.

———. *Celebrating the Single Life*. New York: Doubleday and Co., 1982. rpt: Crossroad, 1990.

———. *Meditation in Motion*. New York: Image Books, 1986.

———. *Pathways of Spiritual Living*. New York: Doubleday and Co., 1984; rpt. Petersham, Mass.: St. Bede's, 1991.

———. *A Practical Guide to Spiritual Reading*. Denville, N.J.: Dimension Books, 1976.

———. *Renewed at Each Awakening: The Formative Power of Sacred Words*. Denville, N.J.: Dimension Books, 1979.

———. *Steps along the Way: The Path of Spiritual Reading*. Denville, N.J.: Dimension Books, 1975.

———. *Womanspirit: Reclaiming the Deep Feminine in Our Human Spirituality*. New York: Crossroad, 1991.

Muto, Susan A., and A. van Kaam. *Commitment: Key to Christian Maturity*. New York: Paulist Press, 1989.

———, and A. van Kaam. *The Emergent Self*. Denville, N.J.: Dimension Books, 1968.

———, and A. van Kaam. *The Participant Self*. Denville, N.J.: Dimension Books, 1969.

———, and A. van Kaam. *Practicing the Prayer of Presence*. Denville, N.J.: Dimension Books, 1980.

———, and A. van Kaam. *Tell Me Who I Am*. Denville, N.J.: Dimension Books, 1977.

Nouwen, Henri J. *The Wounded Healer*. Garden City, N.Y.: Doubleday and Co., 1972.

O'Connor, Flannery. *The Habit of Being*. Ed. Sally Fitzgerald. New York: Farrar, Straus, Giroux, 1979.

O'Donoghue, Noel Dermot. *Heaven in Ordinaire*. Springfield, Ill.: Templegate, 1979.

Ornish, Dean. *Dr. Dean Ornish's Program for Reversing Heart Disease*. New York: Random House, 1990.

Pauling, Linus. *How to Live Longer and Feel Better*. New York: Avon Books, 1986.

Peale, Norman V. *The Power of Positive Thinking*. New York: Prentice-Hall Press, 1968.

———. *Power of the Plus Factor*. New York: Fawcett Crest, 1988.

Pearsall, Paul, Ph.D. *Super Joy*. New York: Bantam Books, 1990.

Pennington, Basil M. *Jubilee: A Monk's Journal*. New York: Paulist Press, 1981.

Peck, M. Scott. *People of the Lie*. New York: Simon & Schuster, 1983.

———. *The Road Less Traveled*. New York: Simon & Schuster, 1978.

Pieper, Josef. *An Anthology*. San Francisco: Ignatius Press, 1984.

———. *Leisure: The Basis of Culture*. Trans. Alexander Dru. New York: New American Library, 1963.

*The Prayers and Meditations of Saint Anselm*. Trans. Sister Benedicta Ward, S.L.G. New York: Penguin Books, 1973.

*The Prison Meditations of Father Delp*. New York: Macmillan, 1963.

*The Pursuit of Wisdom and Other Works*. Trans. James Walsh. New York: Paulist Press, 1988.

Rahner, Hugo. *Man at Play*. New York: Herder & Herder, 1972.

Richard of Saint-Victor. *Selected Writings on Contemplation*. Trans. Clare Kirchberger. New York: Harper and Brothers, 1957.

Rosewell, Pamela. *The Five Silent Years of Corrie ten Boom*. Grand Rapids, Mich.: Zondervan House, 1986.

Schuller, Robert H. *The Be (Happy) Attitudes*. New York: Bantam Books, 1987.

Schumacher, E. F. *Small Is Beautiful*. New York: Harper & Row, 1973.

Segal, Jeanne, Ph.D. *Living beyond Fear*. New York: Ballantine Books, 1989.

Seligman, Martin. *Learned Optimism*. New York: Pocket Books, 1990.

Siegel, Bernie S., M.D. *Love, Medicine, and Miracles*. New York: Harper & Row, 1986.

Steere, Douglas V. *Together in Solitude*. New York: Crossroad, 1985.

ten Boom, Corrie. *The Hiding Place*. London: Hodder & Stoughton, 1971.

———. *Tramp for the Lord*. New York: Pillar Books, 1976.

Teresa of Avila, St. *The Book of Her Life* in *The Collected Works*. Trans. Kieran Kavanaugh, O.C.D., and Otilio Rodriguez, O.C.D. Washington, D.C.: Institute of Carmelite Studies, 1976.

———. *The Interior Castle*. Trans. Kieran Kavanaugh, O.C.D., and Otilio Rodriguez, O.C.D. Classics of Western Spirituality Series. New York: Paulist Press, 1979.

Terkel, Studs. *Working*. New York: Pillar Books, 1976.

Terruwe, Anna A., and Conrad W. Baars. *Psychic Wholeness and Healing*. New York: Alba House, 1981.

Thérèse of Lisieux, St. *Story of a Soul: The Autobiography of St. Thérèse of Lisieux*. Trans. John Clark. Washington, D.C.: Institute of Carmelite Studies, 1975.

Thomas Aquinas, St. *De Anima*. London: Routledge and Kegan Paul, 1951.

————. *Treatise on Happiness*. Trans. John A. Oesterle. Notre Dame, Ind.: University of Notre Dame Press, 1964.

Thoreau, Henry David. *Walden and Civil Disobedience*. Boston: Houghton Mifflin Co., 1960.

Tournier, Paul. *A Place for You: Psychology and Religion*. Trans. Edwin Hudson. London: SCM Press, 1966.

————. *The Whole Person in a Broken World*. Trans. John and Helen Doborstein. New York: Harper & Row, 1964.

Underhill, Evelyn. *Mysticism: A Study in the Nature and Development of Man's Spiritual Consciousness*. London: Methuen and Co., 1949.

————. *Practical Mysticism*. Columbus, Ohio: Ariel Press, 1942.

————. *The Spiritual Life*. Wilton, Conn.: Morehouse-Barlow, 1984.

Vanier, Jean. *Tears of Silence*. Toronto: Griffin House, 1970.

van Kaam, Adrian. *Traditional Formation*. Vol. 5 of *Formative Spirituality*. New York: Crossroad, 1992.

————. *Scientific Formation*. Vol. 4 of *Formative Spirituality*. New York: Crossroad, 1987.

————. *Formation of the Human Heart*. Vol. 3 of *Formative Spirituality*. New York: Crossroad, 1986.

————. *Human Formation*. Vol. 2 of *Formative Spirituality*. New York: Crossroad, 1985.

————. *Fundamental Formation*. Vol. 1 of *Formative Spirituality*. New York: Crossroad, 1983.

————. *Living Creatively*. Denville, N.J.: Dimension Books, 1972.

————. *Looking for Jesus*. Denville, N.J.: Dimension Books, 1978.

————. *Music of Eternity: Everyday Sounds of Fidelity*. Notre Dame, Ind.: Ave Maria Press, 1990.

————. *The Mystery of Transforming Love*. Denville, N.J.: Dimension Books, 1982.

————. *On Being Involved*. Denville, N.J.: Dimension Books, 1970.

———— (co-author with Susan Muto). *Practicing the Prayer of Presence*. Denville, N.J.: Dimension Books, 1980.

————. *Religion and Personality*. Pittsburgh: Epiphany Books, 1991.

————. *Roots of Christian Joy*. Denville, N.J.: Dimension Books, 1985.

————. *Spirituality and the Gentle Life*. Denville, N.J.: Dimension Books, 1974.

———— (co-author with Susan Muto). *Tell Me Who I Am*. Denville, N.J. Dimension Books, 1977.

————. *The Transcendent Self: Formative Spirituality of the Middle, Early, and Late Years of Life*. Pittsburgh: Epiphany Books, 1991.

————. *The Woman at the Well*. Denville, N.J.: Dimension Books, 1976.

von Hildebrand, Dietrich. *Transformation in Christ*. Chicago: Franciscan Herald Press, 1973.

*Webster's New World Dictionary of Quotable Definitions*. Englewood Cliffs, N.J.: Prentice-Hall, 1988.

Wesley, John and Charles. *Selected Writings and Hymns*. Classics of Western Spirituality Series. New York: Paulist Press, 1981.

Wilkes, Paul. *In Mysterious Ways*. New York: Random House, 1990.

Williams, Redford, M.D. *The Trusting Heart*. New York: Times Books, 1989.

Wojcicki, Ed. *A Crisis of Hope in the Modern World*. Chicago: Thomas More Press, 1991.